CULTURES THAT BLOOM

Take Your Organization from Burnout to Balance

CHETNA SETHI, PHD

Copyright © 2026 by Chetna Sethi, PhD

LumiCon Publishing

All rights reserved.

No part of this book may be reproduced in any form or by any electronic or mechanical means, including information storage and retrieval systems, without written permission from the author, except for the use of brief quotations in a book review.

To all those that are silently struggling in jobs they no longer find meaningful - I hope this book will bring hope, courage, and the resolve to live your values.

To all the leaders who are building and growing businesses – I hope there will be a continued commitment to leading with purpose and urgency to prevent burnout.

Contents

Introduction: Is Your Organization Wilting?	1
1. Rubber Bands and the Resilience Myth	14
2. The Culture of "Always On"	27
3. Competing Values, Colliding Cultures	40
4. Embracing Role Clarity and Protecting Boundaries	55
5. Microcultures and the Corner of Discontent	68
6. The Human Cost of Cultural Misalignment	82
7. Redefining Balance	96
8. Meaningful Participation and the Flow State	109
9. Cultures that BLOOM	120
Conclusion: Culture as Leadership Strategy	134
Acknowledgments	149
About the Author	151

Introduction: Is Your Organization Wilting?

It starts with little things. Departments aren't reaching their sales or productivity targets. Direct reports don't respond to messages. There's a sense of low energy around the office and on calls with employees.

Then the situation gets worse. Rumors circulate through the office about how a recent promotion was due to favoritism. A manager tells leadership one thing while telling their team something completely different. People mentally check out in meetings or stop showing up altogether.

These symptoms indicate that your employees are about to burn out, or worse, they may be in burnout already. It's an increasingly common and documented problem. One in four employees surveyed across various demographics around the world report experiencing symptoms of burnout.[1] Even at the C-suite level, nearly 70% of

---

1. McKinsey & Company, "What Is Burnout?" *McKinsey & Company*, August 14, 2023. https://www.mckinsey.com/featured-insights/mckinsey-explainers/what-is-burnout

leaders are seriously considering quitting their jobs in search of positions that better support their wellbeing.[2]

Since the COVID-19 pandemic, and even before that, organizations as a whole and their individual members have been put under more stress than ever before. Employees feel the pressure of ever-growing demands on their time and energy. Many employees have trouble identifying their actual roles and responsibilities or separating their work responsibilities from what needs to be done at home or in other areas of their lives. They feel a pressure to be "always on" as they get buried in endless responsibilities while surrounded by messaging that glorifies a habit of overwork.

People at all levels of different organizations are cracking under the strain. Prolonged stress and unhappiness manifest in organizations as manipulation, rumors, dropped tasks, miscommunication, and an overall toxic work environment. With major technological advancements like AI changing the nature and structures of work, employees have the added stress of job insecurity.

When you finally start to notice these symptoms, you may be at a loss for what steps to take next. You might first identify a single employee as the "problem" and create a performance improvement plan for them. Perhaps you call a town hall meeting to try and identify the reason behind the symptoms you recognize. If you're lucky, you may identify that your employees feel overwhelmed and stretched thin and find ways to start providing them with

---

2. Deloitte, "New Research From Deloitte Finds C-Suite May Soon Join the Great Resignation, Uncovering Well-Being Is a Top-Down Organizational Concern," *PR Newswire*, June 22, 2022. https://www.prnewswire.com/news-releases/new-research-from-deloitte-finds-c-suite-may-soon-join-the-great-resignation-uncovering-well-being-is-a-top-down-organizational-concern-301572794.html

self-care resources. However, simply providing self-care resources to "solve" an organization-wide problem with stress, exhaustion, and dissatisfaction rarely works over the long term.

If you're anything like other leaders I've worked with, you are probably grasping for a solution without fully understanding what is contributing to this decline in your employees' wellbeing. Viewing burnout as a problem to be solved is a blueprint for failure—one that typically emerges from misunderstanding what's *actually* going on when employees start to slide.

What Burnout Is and What It Is Not

By now, burnout is a buzzword. In my work with mid-sized organizations, I've found that people throw the word around without examining what it really means. Often, when asked to define burnout, people recite a list of symptoms or consequences of burnout:

- Overwhelm from a seemingly never-ending to-do list
- Work-induced anxiety
- Feeling "stretched thin" and emotionally drained
- Difficulty concentrating, resulting from a loss of purpose or direction
- Physical symptoms such as headache, fatigue, chest pain, and dizziness
- Having no time for self-care

As familiar as this list has become, it has gotten no closer to actually *defining* burnout. This is a list of symptoms. It is not a description of burnout itself.

When you define something by its symptoms rather than looking at the causes, you are bailing water out of a leaking boat. You might keep everyone afloat for a while, but you're fighting a losing battle. Treating an individual in a vacuum without addressing root causes means that eventually, they will sink, and the whole boat will sink with them.

When people discuss the amount of stress they are under by saying they have "checked out" of their jobs—"quiet quitting" as we now call it—they might be responding to actual burnout. However, most of the time, burnout is the wrong term. In many cases, confusion between the list of symptoms and the actual experience of burnout leads people to believe things are hopeless, even when there is still hope that conditions can improve.

Often people who believe they are in burnout are still successfully bailing water from their boats. They're still afloat, but something more effective needs to happen soon to keep them that way. I call this state "pre-burnout," a state in which a person accumulates stress that seeps into multiple areas of their lives.

If your employees are in pre-burnout, I have good news and bad news.

The good news is, there may still be time to fix the leaky boat. The bad news is that it won't be easy. You are going to have to make some high-level changes before your employees descend from pre-burnout into burnout.

The true definition of burnout is **a state of emotional, physical, and mental exhaustion caused by excessive and prolonged stress**.[3] It sounds extreme, like the way a new parent might be

---

3. Melinda Smith and Sheldon Reid, "Burnout: Symptoms, Treatment, and Coping Strategy Tips," *HelpGuide.org*. Last updated November 14,

pushed to their limits while caring for an infant. It brings to mind sleepless nights and delirious, exhausted days. Such an extreme definition doesn't apply to everyone who reaches the point of burnout. It doesn't have to be a single event that pushes someone beyond what they can handle. It often results from an endless list of pressures that bleed into every area of the person's life.

For some, like the new parent in my example, burnout symptoms might show up as physical exhaustion from long hours of caretaking. For a neurodivergent person, it might manifest as emotional exhaustion from having to mask their authentic self all day, every day. Someone who exhibits perfectionism might become mentally exhausted by the confusion of a job role without clear parameters and boundaries.

A burned-out employee often becomes cynical, and the care they may have once put into their job is replaced with emotional distance. By the time someone is teetering on the edge of burnout, recovery requires extreme individual interventions and very likely an organizational culture shift as well. Once someone reaches this point in whatever position they hold, it's almost impossible to go back. The only option for true healing is leaving the organization or making another dramatic shift, like a move to a different department.

I know this from personal experience because it happened to me. During my time in academia, I experienced pre-burnout for several months before COVID. I was overwhelmed by lesson plans, grading, student meetings, and, of course, my research responsibilities. My life was out of balance, and I had very little time to spend with

---

2025. https://www.helpguide.org/articles/stress/burnout-prevention-and-recovery

my family, but I kept pushing myself to stay on top of my commitments.

At the start of the pandemic, I became pregnant with our first child. Being able to work from home during that period of time was actually helpful; many of my pre-burnout symptoms went away, and I felt rejuvenated even as work continued remotely. However, returning to campus put me right back into the pre-burnout zone. I felt trapped. I couldn't write, I struggled to respond to emails, and the student papers I was reading became harder and harder to comprehend.

We had to send our 11-month-old to daycare because of the return to in-person work. Four weeks later, she came home with COVID and gave it to me and my wife, and all three of us were out for two weeks!

I broke. I crossed the line from pre-burnout to total burnout. I called my boss and let her know I was quitting. That was the beginning of a liberating journey that provided the space to design a life and business that allowed me to live my values.

I was lucky to have enough cushion to quit my job. However, not everyone has the financial security to quit without securing another job in advance, or they don't have the level of power in their organization to draw firm boundaries. Without the autonomy in their job or the flexibility in other areas of their daily life, they trudge along, completely miserable and very likely making the people around them miserable, too.

This is why it is so vital that business leaders strive to create an environment for employees that prevents burnout in the first place. Signs of pre-burnout are canaries in the coal mine. Something in the way a company operates *must* change before it is too late.

Whether you manage teams, work in HR, or have

another type of leadership role, it's up to you to notice the signs before they progress beyond the point of no return. Only then can you act appropriately.

Misunderstanding Burnout

Identifying what burnout really is and how to deal with it is a constant source of confusion to leadership at most organizations. Typically, they hold onto one or more of the following false beliefs:

1. Burnout is a reflection of the individual, and often a sign of weakness.
2. The key sign of burnout is an employee's lowered productivity.
3. Burnout is the problem to be solved.

These false beliefs cause leadership to ask the wrong questions and come to the wrong conclusions. A wellness retreat or workshops about stress management slap a Band-Aid on a gaping wound. These leaders ask themselves, "How do we help employees cope?" when they should be asking, "What systems are driving people to the edge in the first place?"

Think of it this way: imagine you're caring for a flower bed. There is no single factor that makes a flower grow. If you want full and vibrant blossoms, you need to take a number of different factors into account.

First, each plant in the bed needs to be suitable for the environment; a cactus doesn't do so well in a place where there's constant rain, for example. The soil needs to have nutrients, but too much of one nutrient can do its own type of damage as well. Overall, the plant's habitat needs to be welcoming—not choked with weeds—which means each plant should be mostly thriving with room to grow.

Nothing in the garden happens without the ecosystem playing a part. A gardener has to consider how every plant is intricately tied to its environment. One factor being out of balance can result in an entire bed full of struggling plants. Too much sun, not enough water, no fertilizer, or zero weed control can kill off some plants completely.

This more complicated calculus is often overlooked in the corporate version of a flowerbed. Instead many leaders do the equivalent of pouring water onto crispy, dried-out plants, then blame the plants when they don't magically come back to life.

Real gardeners know that dying plants are a signal that something environmental is out of alignment. They also recognize that a few dying plants signal the coming decline of the garden as a whole.

Companies are made up of many individuals. And while the individual may seem to blend in with their peers in the overall organizational chart, companies, like gardens, have complex root systems. Each individual is connected to every other, and what starts in one department will quickly ripple out to impact every other employee.

This is why individual, symptom-based interventions rarely work. Company leadership must instead take a holistic view of organizational health, not only to support the individuals in pre-burnout, but also to contain the issue before it spreads.

My years working 1:1 with everyone from exhausted executives, parents stretched to their limits, and caregivers trying to hold everything together have taught me to take the whole person into consideration. Shifting our understanding of what burnout is in the first place, as well as moving from treating symptoms to addressing causes, results in healthier employees and, by extension, organizations.

With that understanding, I've established a memorable framework to help organizations address burnout at its roots, helping both employees and organizational cultures BLOOM.

The BLOOM Framework

There are measures that can be taken to keep your organization from wilting like a bed full of neglected flowers. The framework below delineates the goal, means to reach that goal, and finally, the outcomes that show you that your efforts have paid off. Using the acronym BLOOM, they consist of the following:

B - Burnout Prevention: A goal that can only be achieved with varied and customized methods.

L - Lifestyle Balance: A means in which an individual is able to put a satisfactory amount of time and energy into different aspects of their lives.

O - Organizational Culture: A means wherein an organization supports each employee to live their values and thrive in cooperation with others.

O - Optimal Quality of Life: The outcome of every individual in an organization being able to meet their needs at work and away from it.

M - Meaningful Participation: The outcome of every individual contributing to their organization in a way that plays into their skills and values.

I use the elements of this framework to measure success at each of my clients' organizations. The data gathered helps us take a methodical approach to preventing burnout before it takes hold. We'll be covering each part of the BLOOM framework and how it can optimize your organization's culture throughout the rest of this book.

B is for Burnout Prevention

Because every individual experiences burnout differently, any measures to prevent burnout must consider an array of personalities and lifestyles. Parents will have different lifestyle-related needs than people without young children. Someone whose personality is more creative and visionary will have different needs than someone who is detail-oriented and analytical. Everyone in the organization will do better with the security of understanding their roles and responsibilities. All these qualities tie into one another and require proactive rather than reactive solutions.

L is for Lifestyle Balance

The term "work-life balance" gives the illusion that work is completely unrelated to the rest of a person's life. In reality, we spend hours and hours at work every week. Work is woven into every part of our lives, and no matter how much we tell people to "leave work at work," that is an unrealistic expectation. For someone to have a balanced lifestyle, they must master the art of adaptability to address their responsibilities more efficiently and effectively in all domains of their life.

Balance looks different to different people, and it's subjective based on a person's current life stage. It doesn't mean that time and effort are evenly distributed across every domain of a person's life at all times. For instance, when someone needs to set aside more time to be a caregiver or when working on a big work-related project, they can still maintain balance by making small adjustments in other areas. Time and energy should be applied where they are most needed. That cannot happen if work is considered separate from life. You will learn about the Balance Mapping tool I use to determine what a balanced life looks like for each person and use it to take stock of your own priorities.

O is for Organizational Culture

Burnout at high levels of an organization trickles down into the lives of its employees. When leaders only prioritize work, they can unknowingly build a culture where employees feel like they must dedicate all their energy to their jobs at the expense of their health and relationships. Leaders can often misjudge the mental state of their employees—if they stop to consider it in the first place. When the values of a particular organization conflict with the actions and behavior of leaders and employees, burnout often follows.

I'll explore what happens when organizations don't live according to their own values, and how that can lead employees to experience cognitive dissonance. I'll also address how important it is for each employee's role to be clarified, from the top down to the lowest levels of an organization. Shifting expectations and blurred boundaries between on and off hours can often result in poor employee wellbeing, which is especially harmful to people experiencing transitions in their lives—things like becoming a parent, buying a house, getting divorced, mourning a loss, or caring for an ill family member.

O is for Optimal Quality of Life

Creating a balanced lifestyle while working at an organization whose culture aligns with your values leads to extraordinary outcomes. If an employee has room to prioritize whatever needs their attention at a given life stage, they are less likely to be pushed to their personal limits. This ideal state doesn't look the same for everyone. However, experiencing security in their work role and finding meaning and purpose in their work activities, all while still having the time to focus on their additional priorities, creates ideal conditions.

Building a company mission and vision that is in alignment with what employees value will result in a sense of satisfaction in all areas of life. I'll demonstrate how centering humans in an organization's mission, vision, and policies can elevate that organization's culture.

M is for Meaningful Participation

It takes much more energy to complete unclear tasks than ones that are well-defined and have a visibly positive result. When people have a sense of purpose in their work, they are more likely to become fully present in the moment. That's a key element in mindfulness practice and can often unlock a flow state—where the employee is completely absorbed in the task at hand. Flow states benefit the human brain and can even be considered a form of self-care.

However, meaningful participation goes beyond simply executing a task and feeling satisfied. It also gives employees (and leaders too) a reason to get out of bed in the morning and go to work. The sum of each task they do helps contribute to their sense of productivity, and even further than that, their sense of meaning.

Achieving a Culture of Balance

It is possible to stop burnout within organizations before it starts. Building a positive culture, which accounts for the many factors that influence burnout, begins with a focus on wellness rather than performance.

Starting with wellness means you are looking at causes and not just symptoms. You are helping people feel secure in their roles and understanding of why they do what they do. You consider people's values and what type of accommodations they need in their daily lives in order to reach an optimal quality of life.

When all those things come together, your organization will have greater employee satisfaction, better retention, and cohesive teams that function better together.

In the coming chapters, we'll identify the red flags signaling that your employees are burning out and that you need to make some changes to your organizational culture. Then, I'll share some leadership strategies that will help keep your culture aligned with your organization's values and those of your employees.

If you're watching your organization slide into burnout, it's not too late to get on the right track. Reading about the true impacts of a culture of burnout in the coming chapters will help you build a healthier organization and a culture of balance, where everyone can blossom together.

1

Rubber Bands and the Resilience Myth

Imagine a rubber band. Some rubber bands can stretch to great lengths without breaking, returning to their original shape and form after being placed under the stress of being pulled taut. The rubber band can be used again and again, each time returning to its neutral state, ready to be stretched again. The more it is capable of stretching, the more it is considered *resilient*.

Often human resilience is compared to rubber bands. The more a person can stretch and strain and reach while still rebounding—apparently with ease—the more resilient they are said to be. In the working world, resilience is something that heads of organizations look for in their employees. Why wouldn't they? According to basic logic, an employee who is more resilient can accomplish more, especially under pressure.

Because the answer seems so simple, many leaders stop here. They conclude that you should only employ those who can stretch the furthest—over and over—without breaking. In this way of thinking, those who can't stretch as far lack resilience and, therefore, the capacity to perform under pressure. If they burn out, it's simply a sign they couldn't handle their job, and the organization would be better off without them.

However, if you take basic logic a step further, you'll see the problem with the rubber band analogy—a rubber band that is constantly stretched to its limit will weaken over time. If the rubber band is always stretched as far as possible, it will eventually snap, no matter how strong it is to begin with.

Leadership often expects people to stretch, forgetting that even rubber bands need time to relax. Putting pressure on individuals to build resilience and manage their own stress, without relieving any of the stressors themselves, is much easier than changing systems within the organization.

When leaders think of stress as a problem with the individual—a rubber band that lacks the ability to stretch—they may even reduce the issue to a "morale problem." Minor interventions are often added to the employee's workday; they may start by hosting workshops about "work-life balance" (an inaccurate term I will address later in this book). They may conduct anonymous surveys, which frequently have low response rates and whose results are never meaningful enough to help leaders identify effective action steps. They may offer an Employee Assistance Program as a solution or design after-work social activities that are unpaid and only optional on paper. When employees have been stretched too thin, usually repeatedly, additional hoops prevent the rest necessary to return to a relaxed state. Even worse, these band-aid leadership "solutions" actually become part of the problem. If someone is constantly stretched too far, office happy hours won't help. They won't even be fun.

No matter how high an employee's stress tolerance may

be, the constant tension between expectations and necessary rest can wreak havoc on their lives. Sure, some people are able to cope without burning out, but this is usually only temporary. Once an employee has been stretched to their limits, any additional stretching threatens to cause that final snap. No matter how resilient they are, when a person snaps, they can't return to what they were before. Once the elasticity gives out, you're left with a broken rubber band.

Stretched but Not Broken

Stress is messy, and its causes are rarely confined to one domain of life. When I am called into an organization, I find that employees are typically on a spectrum from slightly stretched to just short of snapping. This is usually when the word "burnout" enters the scene, as many employees use it to incorrectly define symptoms of stress in their lives. However, the experience of ongoing stress—even extreme ongoing stress—does not necessarily equate to a state of burnout. In most cases, these employees are not describing burnout itself, but a concept I call pre-burnout.

A lot of what distinguishes pre-burnout from full-fledged burnout is how stressors overlap across the different areas of an individual's life. Pre-burnout can start with prolonged stress in just one domain and can be as extreme as that stress bleeding into different domains of life, such as the person's work, home, or social life. Personal characteristics can make someone more or less prone to symptoms of pre-burnout. If someone has a tranquil home life and a laid-back, go-with-the-flow personality, they may be less affected by stressors at work. Even if work is stressful, if they somehow manage to completely unplug when they get home, they have the opportunity to release tension. To use the rubber band metaphor, they can save their elasticity for when they return to work.

However, for those whose personality tends to be more prone to anxiety, it may be hard for them to switch their working brain off when they're not at the office. They sleep badly, create rifts between themselves and loved ones, and reach for unhealthy coping mechanisms. If they are under stress in their home life—family members to care for or a strained relationship with their partner, for example—that rubber band will stay stretched out at all hours of the day. It's all the worse if they have unique stressors in every domain, which is the case for many people.

Pre-burnout is almost inevitable when work stress crosses boundaries or when other stressors start affecting your work. And this almost always happens. It's rare for stress to be isolated to either one's work or home, and stressors that tangle together keep people over-extended, living an unsustainable lifestyle that will eventually break them.

Stretching in one domain of life means stretching in others as well, no matter what measures one takes. An employee can try to make their home environment as peaceful as possible, start a yoga practice to relax their anxious mind, and take frequent breaks at work between high-pressure meetings. These practices may be helpful, despite being stacked on top of an already overly stressful work environment, but this does not offset the elements of their life that are beyond their control. No one can deep-breathe their way out of an overloaded to-do list or toxic interactions with coworkers. No matter how peaceful they make their bedtime routine, these unaddressed factors are bound to creep in. Once the stressors begin to overshadow factors beyond their control, the rubber band stops returning to its original size. Most people will eventually snap.

I have worked with people on both ends of the spectrum, but my favorite part about my job is working with people before they break, when there is hope for building personal and organizational adaptability to relieve pre-burnout and address organizational dysfunction. Bringing people back to a state of relaxation is a matter of leaders recognizing signs of burnout, identifying areas where stress can be curtailed, and then setting up systemic interventions.

The Real Causes of Pre-Burnout

The root of all pre-burnout in an organization is misalignment, or more accurately multiple misalignments. Misalignments occur both at the individual and organizational level—sometimes an individual's values misalign with the way the organization operates; other times, the organization operates in a way that is misaligned with its own values; though often, both occur simultaneously. These misalignments amplify each other, chronically stretching people beyond what they can comfortably handle, while silently perpetuating the culture of burnout.

Portrait of a Life in Pre-Burnout

Imagine a day in the life of an employee who is in a state of pre-burnout. We'll call her Maria. She has been experiencing excessive fatigue, headaches, irritability at work and home, and a lack of concentration due to poor sleep.

Maria wakes up to her alarm clock after sleeping badly; the many thoughts running through her head don't allow her to rest. A frustrating work project just seems to drag on and on as the scope keeps changing, and she feels like she's doing the work of multiple people on her team. One of her two kids is getting bullied, and she's been called by the school more than once, which has eaten into the time when she should be working.

Fortunately, she has a hybrid position, and today she gets to work from home. Since Maria is an introvert, she has a much easier time being productive when she can work by herself. The noise of the office drains her and keeps her from tackling her ever-growing to-do list.

However, the first thing that she sees in the company's Slack channel after dropping the kids off at school is that her team will be required to come into the office tomorrow and every day over the next week. She has a rush of adrenaline as she realizes she'll have to scramble to find someone to watch the kids when they're done with school. Her parents sometimes take that role, but they're out of town this week, so she'll have to place an unknown number of calls to find childcare today—without sacrificing her work tasks of course.

Because Maria is also very conscientious, she beats herself up, quite unfairly, for not having been ready for this scenario. She's supposed to have a predictable schedule of workplace locations, but those goalposts move constantly. It doesn't help that she can never pin down her supervisor to get the clarity she needs to complete her projects.

Just as Maria is breaking for lunch, one of her coworkers calls her. Maria quickly eats her sandwich while her coworker spends the time complaining about their department supervisor. It takes Maria a lot of emotional energy to navigate her coworker's feelings, and even though she shares her coworker's frustrations, the conversation only makes her feel worse. After hanging up, she's so tightly wound that she can't focus on what she planned to get done today.

When her supervisor does check in with her for the first time in over a week, it's through an urgent email sent five minutes before she has to leave to pick up her kids from school. The supervisor doesn't bother to mask his annoyance when she takes over an hour to respond, even though her daily routine was approved by management. As far as the supervisor is concerned, work should be Maria's highest priority—after all, *he* stays late every day to complete his projects. Why can't Maria be that driven, too?

By the end of the day, Maria's head is pounding, and she has a tight feeling in her chest that makes it difficult to breathe. But there is no time to deal with those problems because she has errands to run. She pops a couple of ibuprofen for the headache, so she can get everything done before the shops close.

Even worse, Maria snaps at her kids over minor things from the time she picks them up to the time they go to bed. She feels like she's failing as a mother when she has problems helping them with their homework or makes boxed mac and cheese for dinner instead of a healthier meal. When her spouse comes home, she snaps at him too. She feels unsupported, but even when she gets help, it never feels like enough to keep her head above water.

At the end of the night, after the kids are in bed, she stays up too late watching home-improvement shows and drinking more wine than she intends. She feels guilty, but it's the only time she gets to herself all day. And, of course, she sleeps badly again.

Many organizations would attribute Maria's low energy to her poor sleep and alcohol consumption, ignoring everything that came before and actually caused those issues. After all, the thinking goes, there is plenty of scientific and anecdotal evidence that links alcohol and poor sleep, and poor sleep obviously leads to low energy. If only she'd implement a healthier sleep schedule, she would build up her resilience, making work expectations a breeze.

Unfortunately, Maria's problems won't be solved by replacing her unhealthy bedtime ritual. Even if she stopped drinking wine and enforced a strict bedtime, that wouldn't solve the multiple other stressors that come from her work life, home life, and the way she naturally relates to the world. Some might say that these are normal stressors that a stronger, more resilient employee would be able to handle. However, when we consider the rates of burnout in the working population, it becomes clear that categorizing situations like Maria's as "normal" is undoubtedly part of the problem.

Recognizing Pre-Burnout in Individuals

Signs of pre-burnout are often clearest when employees are considered individually. People in pre-burnout become anxious and irritable; they complain about how busy they are and how they constantly feel behind in their work; they make mistakes or are late with assignments. Even chronic health problems like headaches and stomach problems can be indicators of pre-burnout.

However, pre-burnout in the workplace cannot be fully understood by considering the employee in isolation, because pre-burnout is an issue of misalignment. Misalignment between an individual and an organization happens when the organization's demands make a person operate out of sync with their own values. For example, Maria has always wanted to prioritize family time, but work stressors leave her a frazzled mess by the end of the day, and she is unable to be with her family the way she wants. These feelings lead her to lash out at her family in a way that makes her feel guilty and lowers her self-esteem.

Maria's image of who she wants to be is at odds with who she is. If her job makes it impossible for her to embody the partner and parent she wants to be, then even if she leaves the office promptly at five, the stress of her job is bleeding into her home life. In order for her to reach alignment with herself, her relationship with her job needs to change. But how can it change when the things that make it so frustrating are outside her control?

People (who are financially able to) typically quit their jobs at this stage. That leads to high turnover, which should be a red flag for management of things to come. If they decide to stay, like Maria, they will remain misaligned with their own values and stretch even further. Soon, they will feel trapped in their positions; any satisfaction they once got from their jobs will vanish, and they will find themselves unable to tap into even the most basic motivations for completing their assigned tasks. They will struggle to find purpose in every task they complete, making the job feel even less meaningful. If things continue the way they are, they will eventually cross over from pre-burnout to burnout.

Recognizing Pre-Burnout in Your Organization

Individual behavior is not the only indicator of burnout. Leaders often first become aware of burnout when their organization begins to malfunction, frequently because leaders are oblivious to the signs of misalignment.

When pre-burnout becomes an epidemic within an organization, leaders may recognize the following symptoms:

- **Conflicting reports:** discrepancies between what different individuals or departments report to leadership.
- **Unmet targets:** multiple people not delivering the work they're supposed to have done, even if they look busy all the time.
- **Gossip and cliques:** groups start to see one another as adversaries and spread gossip or complaints about one another.
- **High turnover:** people leave the organization altogether more quickly than they used to.
- **Communication silos:** different departments shut themselves off from the rest of the company, leading to misunderstandings and things slipping through the cracks.
- **Low morale:** employees aren't engaged in their work, either missing their targets completely or simply going through the motions.

If you see any of these symptoms in your organization, something is wrong with your systems. Even if you only notice one person suffering due to individual indicators, other employees may simply have a temperament that causes them to endure the stretch for longer times or display different symptoms of pre-burnout that may not be overtly visible yet. That doesn't mean they won't eventually break as well.

Reframing Burnout from Individuals to Systems

People who don't recognize burnout as a systemic issue are more likely to fall prey to two of the biggest misconceptions about burnout—that it is a problem to be solved, and that it's completely within the control of the individual. The focus on employee resilience places limitations on problem-solving, suppresses innovation, and stands in the way of learning. Placing all the burden on individuals is a temporary and typically ineffective intervention—individuals cannot solve systemic issues, especially when they are buried in misalignment.

However, while individual interventions almost always fail, surveying and truly listening to employees is an important first step to building systems that support employees and prevent burnout.

Talk to the people who show symptoms of misalignment and pre-burnout: On a scale of 1 to 10, how stressed do they feel? What stresses them out most in their jobs? Are they deriving any pleasure or meaning from what they do? Often they will describe their situation as being overly stressed or stretched too thin, but the symptoms they are experiencing are often pre-burnout symptoms.

Employees may also use the word burnout as a buzzword since it has now become synonymous with "overworked and underpaid." This points to society's work culture in general, as it is more and more common for people to hold two to three jobs just to pay rent. The growing rates of self-reported burnout due to economic hardship and higher costs of living are not always from toxic work environments and can't necessarily be addressed within the scope of the workplace. However, eliminating organization-wide problems is within the scope of leadership's control.

Those in top leadership at a company don't always recognize these issues on their own. The good news is that emerging leaders within HR or hired consultants may eventually be able to hold up a mirror to help them recognize both misaligned values within the organization itself as well as ones between employees and the organization. Listening to this feedback and acknowledging those misalignments will eventually help leaders zoom out and see where things can be improved.

Stop Pre-Burnout Before Your Employees Break

Looking for systemic stressors in your workplace is a multi-part process. While pre-burnout can ripple through a company's staff, it affects different people to varying levels. In the following chapters, you'll learn to recognize and address some of the most common root causes of burnout.

First, take account of **boundary blurring.** Are there areas where work is negatively impacting an employee's other life domains? Maybe their department's culture interferes with their ability to take advantage of the work-from-home policy, causing marginalization of employees. Maybe they are expected to answer calls or messages after hours, taking them away from family dinners or bedtime rituals. Maybe they are expected to do work that is outside of their job description.

Next, observe whether there is **low employee autonomy**. Are your employees equipped with the decision-making skills they need when a supervisor is not available or accessible? If employees are unable to do the work they need to do without the input of a supervisor, especially an uncommunicative or overly critical supervisor, they may feel powerless and lose a meaningful connection to their work. This is demoralizing for many, and it will zap any feeling of job satisfaction they may have had before they reached pre-burnout.

Finally, and perhaps most importantly, evaluate **lead-**

ership team behavior. What kind of behavior do leaders model for the rest of the company? A culture of overwork may exhaust people who believe they need to keep up or risk losing their jobs. It also might lead to employees feeling that there is no way to accommodate the demands of their lives outside of work. Remember, a culture of burnout flows from the top!

Additional factors that I like to call **wild cards** will be discussed throughout the book as well. Some examples include inflexibility that makes employees feel like they can't effectively manage multiple responsibilities outside work; job insecurity that leads to employees not taking Paid Time Off (PTO) out of fear that they will be made redundant or worse, their role will be eliminated all together; or communication silos that lead to isolation and a lack of trust both among employees and towards leadership.

Resilience training on its own will not solve the pre-burnout problem in your organization. It isn't enough to send out an email with a list of healthy coping mechanisms or to conduct one-on-one listening sessions designed to give stress management tips to suffering employees. When you search through the lens of misalignment rather than individual resilience, the symptoms you see in your organization—both up close and zoomed out—will make it clear that systemic change is required. In the following chapters, I'll share different areas for improvement within your organization to minimize pre-burnout with the goal of helping you create cultural change. When you target the systems that stretch employees too thin, you'll not only help those in pre-burnout find rest and restoration—you'll also improve outcomes, turnover, and general workplace happiness. That should help everyone sleep better at night.

2

The Culture of "Always On"

The normalization of work-from-home during the height of the COVID-19 pandemic was transformative. Employees stopped going to the office and set up workspaces wherever was convenient. Kitchen tables became conference tables. Children's playrooms became Zoom booths. No matter what space became a home office, a person's home-based responsibilities were constantly visible. Showing up as your "authentic self" had a brand new, much more literal meaning. People could continue with their jobs while remaining available to take care of things at home when necessary (and vice versa).

Some people thrive in this type of environment, particularly those who don't struggle as much when asked to quickly shift between tasks. They are more comfortable with splitting their attention between sending an email before feeding their kids lunch or folding laundry while on a work call. They thrive when juggling housekeeping, caregiving, and contributing at work. For others, the effect is more complicated; they feel uncertain of what is expected of them and often feel pulled in different directions.

Regardless of how suited an individual is to this new way of operating, the fact remains that work-from-home blurred boundaries for organizations and their employees. It erased the line between workspaces and home spaces. The blend of expectations in these two formerly separate domains overwhelmed those who were used to compartmentalizing—competing values now literally occupied the same space. Work-from-home encourages permeability of both physical boundaries and emotional ones, and boundary erosion is one of the most persistent drivers of lifestyle imbalance and, eventually, burnout.

Many organizations have required their staff to return to the office either full time or in hybrid form, but work-from-home is here to stay, and the dividing lines between physical spaces and between emotional boundaries remain blurred. That new normal was built on technological infrastructure that was developed to accommodate the demands of work during the pandemic. It also encouraged different social norms around work, which were adjusted to make room for this new way of living.

With remote work, managing office space and technology falls more on the shoulders of individuals. It is up to them to maintain boundaries between work and home, and they are responsible for shifting between differing roles throughout the day. In a healthy organization, it's much easier for employees to find a balance that works for everyone. However, when the brunt of boundary management is left up to individual resilience within a possibly toxic work culture, organizations run the risk of running employees into the ground.

Technology That Never Sleeps and Shifting Availability Demands

These days, encroachment on an individual's space is powered by greater digital accessibility. It used to be that "taking work home with you" was a literal act, where a person transported work materials from their offices to their homes. Once upon a time, even work email and shared drives were impossible for people to access anywhere but at the office. The work-from-home requirements of COVID triggered a boom in the development of cloud-based technologies, which now allow people to access email, shared drives, messaging applications, and project management software from anywhere they can connect to the internet.

In addition to tools that speed up communication, many employees of large organizations no longer reliably have designated work phones; they now find themselves using their personal devices to make business calls and send messages. Similarly, not every worker has an organization-supplied computer, necessitating the use of personal computers for work-focused tasks. Personal projects and communications commingle with work responsibilities in an individual's digital ecosystem.

The technological innovations we now have access to come with a double edge. There's the opportunity to work where one chooses and better collaborate with geographically diverse teams, but with it comes higher expectations that an employee be constantly online—or "always on." Since it is now so easy to check messages or "hop on a quick call" at any moment, expectations for how people engage with work are expanding and gaining speed. If an employee is technically off work, even a small allowance, such as responding to a short email, can break the dam for work to flood into every area of their life.

"Always-on" culture makes it so when an employee sees an email come in, they feel obligated to respond in the same way one might reply to a text message: immediately. If someone sees a notification on a Saturday afternoon, their mind may not allow them to rest until they've taken action; what might start as answering a quick question may result in the employee opening their computer to spend an hour on an ongoing project. Meanwhile, they've interrupted time with their families or other responsibilities to sneak off and get work done.

This is especially a risk for generations who were raised within a more tech-heavy environment, where instant gratification is the norm. Today's workers tend to come from family systems where they were expected to be accessible via cell phone starting at a very young age. For those who are used to constant availability to parents, the transition to constant availability to a boss feels natural; with no clear divisions between home and the workplace, any time or place is fair game.

The Negative Effects of "Always-On" Culture

Misalignment within a company culture takes a toll on employees' individual lives, and that can hurt an entire organization's ability to perform well. Lacking separation between one's professional and personal lives often weakens an individual's commitment to both, and their engagement with all domains of life can suffer as a result. Blurred boundaries can have dire effects; in addition to weakening an employee's performance at work, weakened (or fully demolished) boundaries can cause chaos within their schedules and damage their health. That alteration may silently reshape their behavior in ways that feel increasingly out of sync.

Physical boundaries allow people to mentally transition from one role to another with greater ease. They walk out of one building and shed whatever persona they were wearing in that space, and they have time to transition to whichever is called for at their destination. Don't get me wrong, I'm not implying that people are wearing masks and need to constantly hide their true selves in every setting. Instead, they are likely making transitions based on the microculture they are leaving and towards norms of the microculture they are entering (a concept I will explain in more depth later). When there is no space to make a clear transition between physical spaces, it's very difficult to fully embody a single role. One's identities—professional, parent, partner, or a community leader—all blend together in ways that are sure to have conflicting demands, leading to that rubber band being in a chronically stretched state.

While many people are comfortable with multi-tasking, this approach is rarely conducive to high work performance. Repeated task-switching makes extra demands on a person's executive function and eats up time and energy. Moving back and forth between different behavioral dynamics takes a lot of energy to sustain, and when there is no true focus on either role, individuals find themselves drained of their ability to perform both. Quickly moving from making lunch for the family to writing up a work report often feels like running a mental obstacle course, resulting in the same fatigue.

Activities like responding to emails at midnight, texting your boss over the weekend, and answering Slack messages during dinner might seem like no big deal at first—they are just bad habits—but they do serious damage over time.

Those behaviors are part of a culture that equates availability for work with one's commitment to it, and always being ready to respond to work demands is an emotional strain that keeps an individual stretched like our proverbial rubber band.

An "always-on' mentality prevents employees from sleeping soundly, taking breaks throughout their workday, or using their paid time off. They feel as if going on vacation is no excuse to break their connection to work, an attitude that affects one's brain and physiology. Conflicting demands that can show up at any time of the day or night rewire people's brains. Chronic unease that comes from waiting for urgent demands from work can form a direct line to illness, making an endless state of hypervigilance a precursor to burnout.

When work and home inhabit the same physical space, the employee may find it difficult to disconnect their work from their worth. Relaxing can feel impossible at home, since home is now a space that is synonymous with productivity. When people cannot disconnect, they have no time for reflection or processing. They feel the need to be ready to perform for others and respond to work demands at any time, day or night.

When the walls come down between work, home, and a person's core values, it also erodes trust between the employee and the organization. There is no longer any security in the fact that time off is *actual* time off. Employees become prone to reactivity and anxiety, because they know that, at any moment, they could be called upon to jump into action. Unfortunately, if an organization expects its employees to be "always on," this feeling of being on edge 24/7 may be justified. Whether or not it's fair or even technically allowed, employees can be punished for not conforming to a toxic organizational culture.

When Workplace Availability Norms Become Toxic

As a Forbes Coaches Council member, I am often asked to provide my expert opinion on organizational issues. During one panel, I was asked for innovative ways the C-suite could support employee caregivers. Immediately, my head began to buzz with flexible policies that leadership could put in place to encourage a balanced lifestyle for employees trying to manage their caregiving responsibilities with their work.

Then I started looking at responses from the other panel members, and I realized they were giving similar suggestions —strategies like adding employee resource groups (ERGs) that host special coffee hours for parents or writing policies designed to give flexible hours to those with caregiving duties. If these ideas were so common and came recommended by so many experts, it followed that most companies would already have such policies in place. However, if people were repeatedly receiving these recommendations, writing them into policy, and then forgetting about them, the initiatives would never work. These supports can significantly reduce stress, increase job satisfaction, and help retain top talent, but only if organizations promote and encourage their use.

Most organizations have official policies in place that technically lay down boundaries between when people are "on" or "off." Written rules may confine work communication to business hours only, but unwritten rules within organizations can challenge them. An organization that doesn't follow its own rules creates an additional source of ambiguity and blurred boundaries, and employees can become more stressed and disengaged as a result.

When "I didn't get any sleep last night because I was so busy working on this project" earns applause from coworkers and management, it establishes a dangerous precedent. A culture that celebrates high productivity, then conflates it with workaholism, sends a more powerful message than any written policy at an organization. There may be policies that allow people to take time off, but that culture makes some afraid to use it.

This isn't just speculation. According to a study released in 2023, between 46% and 51% of employees at all levels of an organization do not take all their allotted paid time off. Employees within this bracket give their reasons:

- not feeling like they need the time off (52%),
- concerns they will fall behind in their work (49%),
- feeling badly that their coworkers will need to take on additional work (43%);
- fears that they will hurt their chances of advancement in the organization (indicative of a toxic work culture) (19%),
- fears that they might risk losing their job (16%), or
- they are discouraged from doing so by management (12%).[1]

Those who have no choice but to use work-sanctioned

---

1. Shradha Dinesh and Kim Parker, "More Than 4 in 10 U.S. Workers Don't Take All Their Paid Time Off," *Pew Research Center*, August 10, 2023. https://www.pewresearch.org/short-reads/2023/08/10/more-than-4-in-10-u-s-workers-dont-take-all-their-paid-time-off/

flexibility are often the test cases that prove those fears valid. These people are going through transitional seasons in their lives, spaces in which their needs and values go through changes. Examples include those caring for someone who is chronically ill, having a baby, buying a house, getting divorced, or moving an elderly parent into the home. In a culture that values productivity over everything else, employees in transition are often the test cases that demonstrate whether the organization is supporting the use of their own policies or merely tolerating them.

When Leadership Models an "Always-On" Culture

There is evidence that the pressure to work overtime and not take advantage of paid (or even unpaid) time off is even more rampant in the C-suite than in lower levels of an organization. One study found that one in four executives were afraid to take time off at the risk of getting too far behind their work, while 24% of executives worried they would miss important messages or emails if they disconnected.

Personally, I have encountered CEOs who have had to make a great effort to stop and take real breaks from their work. One CEO in particular, who invited me to speak about lifestyle balance with his employees, found it extremely difficult to disconnect from his job, even when he went on vacation. While he has since come around, he said that he thought of the company as "his baby." For him that meant he still had to be in on every piece of communication that passed through his inbox until he finally trained himself to hand over control to another executive.

His own words demonstrate just how much an executive's difficulty unplugging from work can trickle down to the rest of the organization. It's a paternalistic style of management that naturally casts employees in the role of children who use leaders as examples of the way they should behave. For those whose lifestyle doesn't allow them to be "always on," there are very real concerns that they'll face repercussions if they cannot keep up.

How "Always-On" Culture Marginalizes Employees

When employees express fears over taking time off, they are not being dramatic. People who need flexibility at work, or find themselves marginalized in other areas of their lives, are often more anxious about using their PTO or using flexible policies offered by their employers based on guilt and fear. The aforementioned Pew study also found that women are more likely to cite concerns over their coworkers having to take on more work, and Black employees are more likely than white employees to say that they are afraid they'll lose their jobs if they take time off. Employees of all races and genders who have been with their employer for less than a year, or between one and five years, also express the same job insecurity. In fact, the 2024 median reported job tenure in the United States at just 4.2 years; this is not an insignificant number.

The Family and Medical Leave Act (FMLA) entitles employees to unpaid, job-protected leave for up to twelve weeks, but just because employees have access to it doesn't mean they can't expect repercussions to using it. For example, there are cases where women have returned to work after maternity leave to find themselves excluded from the former leadership roles they had once enjoyed. Because they exercised their legal rights to focus on a transitional period in their lives, they felt they had to rebuild their credibility from scratch.

A major cause of burnout comes from a lack of autonomy at work. It stresses employees out when they feel like they cannot get ahead no matter what they do or that they are being punished for having needs outside of work. Over time, these feelings of helplessness can suck the joy out of their work and cause them to burn out. It's a lose-lose scenario. The persistent stretch of being "always on" and the punishment for not being "always on" both lead to the same place: burnout. The only cure is to improve organizational culture.

Unplugging from an "Always-On" Mentality

The new normal includes remote and hybrid work, and it's unlikely that every workplace will return to the old ways of operating. Employees and organizations must now find new ways to define the boundaries between work and home, both between the physical spaces and between the associated emotional states.

One way that individuals can break from being "always on" is by changing their relationship with technology. Relegating certain digital spaces to work alone can draw a line between business time and leisure time. Individuals can log out of their work email and messaging systems when work hours are over, then reinforce boundaries using away messages, delayed sending features, status indicators, or autoresponders reminding people that they don't respond during their off hours. Areas of the home can be dedicated specifically to work, and the employee can make a solid rule that when they get up from their desk at the end of the day, they don't go back.

However, none of these safeguards will work without one key factor: cooperation with the rest of the organization. For individuals to be able to enforce healthy boundaries, the organization must be prepared to back them up. Support cannot stop at offering benefits on paper. Even the best-designed and well-intentioned policies will fall flat if they are not prioritized by leadership and upheld by all employees.

Leaders need to shift from merely tolerating people's right to boundaries to actively encouraging them. If only one employee of the organization reinforces their boundaries, they become out of sync with the rest of the organization, and the company culture may sideline them or cause others to see them as "difficult." When flexibility is viewed with suspicion, employees may shy away from resources that can lead to achieving balance. It's an excellent way to drive an organization's best employees into burnout.

The Rewards of Solid Boundaries

Those who keep boundaries somewhat permeable are in the majority. This is understandable as permeable boundaries can promote flexibility, support balancing different areas of life, and even encourage an individual to show up in all areas of life as their authentic self. But let's face it, while permeable boundaries are healthy, we all have moments when these boundaries get blurred or even erased. Those who keep boundaries not just flexible but consistently blurred are at the highest risk of burnout. Both individuals and organizations benefit from boundary protection. It gives individuals the freedom to manage their routines and dedicate their full attention to whatever role they are playing in the moment. Their freedom benefits the organization because the workers are more refreshed, relaxed, and focused on their work tasks.

When there are clear boundaries around work hours, individuals can give their full energy and attention to their work rather than disappearing at unpredictable times throughout the day and becoming distracted. For some, this can mean working late into the night while lying in bed, for others it may mean a strict 9 to 5 schedule. Regardless of what personal boundaries look like for each team, team members have better clarity about when they can expect answers to questions or the best times to reach out. Working with clear boundaries also requires a more organized and well-planned approach to projects, banishing panicked off-hours messages. Lower rates of reactivity and anxiety will give employees the clear-headedness they need to fully engage with work and collaborate more effectively.

Restructuring norms provides clarity to individuals, their coworkers, and leadership. Employees can find comfort in knowing exactly when their energy and attention is needed at work and when they can recharge and attend to their needs outside of work. That balance lets them separate both their physical spaces and their emotional spaces, relieving them of the burden of having to juggle all their roles, values, and expectations all at once.

3

Competing Values, Colliding Cultures

On paper, your organization may look immune to employee burnout. You have an employee handbook that clearly states what you're all about. Your company's mission, vision, and core values are clearly stated on your website and easily discoverable. You may offer generous Paid Time Off (PTO), set guidelines for employees' working hours, and have a clearly written diversity, equity, and inclusion (DEI) statement posted on your website. Perhaps you have even launched cultural initiatives designed to promote wellbeing and trust within your organization.

Research on organizational culture has verified what many employees recognize intuitively: making pronouncements about culture doesn't always reflect the real experience of working at an organization. In fact, in a survey across organizations that launched cultural initiatives in 2022, 72% of them did not show any positive gains in employee trust, engagement, and retention after a year.[1]

---

1. Benjamin Laker, Chidiebere Ogbonnaya, Yasin Rofcanin, Tomasz

Announcements and new policies were simply not enough to create a new reality at the participating companies.

So what if, despite your policy efforts, you still see signs of trouble in your organization? When employee initiatives don't work, it's time to look at systems. When you zoom out to view the entirety of your organization, are you certain that it's living up to its own stated standards?

The key lies in the difference between philosophy and action. Even if your organization has a full set of company policies, the scripts people actually follow may be quite different. As we discussed with "always on" culture, while employees may have access to PTO, they may feel pressured not to use it. Restrictions on working hours can coexist with a shadow-culture of overwork that blows past those rules. Whether you have a stated DEI policy or not, what employees notice and remember is what actually happens when someone reports microaggressions.

People at the executive level often don't realize how much their employees are struggling. Often, leadership is not as in touch with employees as they believe. Other times, employees feel pressured to put on a positive front for executives, even when they feel completely disconnected from organizational values. This is where culture comes into play. If there's a misalignment between leaders' perception of employee behavior and the employees' actual experience of the workplace, the weak spot is almost always organizational culture.

Gorny, and Marcello Mariani, "To Change Company Culture, Focus on Systems—Not Communication," *Harvard Business Review*, August 25, 2025. https://hbr.org/2025/08/to-change-company-culture-focus-on-systems-not-communication

Where Misalignments Show Up

Many organizations have policies in place that are meant to help employees balance their lives and find meaning in their work. If the policies are out of alignment with what is really going on in the organization, it can stress employees out so significantly that they are pushed farther down the path toward burnout.

While we've discussed "Always-on" culture as a potential source of misalignment, it is far from the only cause. Organizational culture influences every aspect of a company's work environment. It extends to structures of accountability, employees' ability to protect their own boundaries and make their own choices, and the organization's openness to adapt. Cultural realignment is about connecting an organization's vision and core values with every single person who works there, no matter their role, so that every member of the team can find passion and meaning in their work. As valuable as it can be to align organizational culture with employee experience, the inverse is just as damaging. When the culture is out of alignment, the company suffers measurably along with its employees.

Since individual personal needs differ, misalignment affects each employee differently. Some people may be comfortable with focusing primarily on company needs. They are focused on the product or service the company provides and derive deep satisfaction from the work itself. However, if the organization only values this type of work-centered "go-getter," anyone with other needs is likely to feel disconnected at best and marginalized at worst.

If work repeatedly clashes with an employee's priorities day after day, it wears the employee down like waves eroding a cliffside. In my interviews with employees of the organizations I work with, I find that most of them started out enthusiastic about their company's stated values when they were hired. However, even people who agree with the company's mission and vision with all their hearts can start hating their jobs. When the values they signed on to uphold aren't evident in the company's actions, the employee is more likely to burn out. If you take the time to evaluate organizational culture, you stand a chance of stopping burnout before you lose the load-bearing pillars of your company: your employees.

A successful organizational culture shows up when the organization's vision and mission are lived out through employees' everyday actions at every level. Organizational values that misalign with an employee's way of operating in the world will start ripping at the seam between them and their workplace. Building an organization that upholds its own values cannot be a one-and-done approach, because creating policies is not the same as creating a culture. Effectively addressing the need for alignment with employees requires organizations to learn adaptability and to be intentional with the way their cultures are built.

Organizational culture can only thrive when it acknowledges the simple fact that employees bring their own cultures into the workplace every day. Each person's values, family roles, and ways of operating in the world shape how they experience the job. An organization that assumes everyone will thrive under the same set of expectations will quickly run into resistance. What energizes one person may drain another. For example, a culture that prizes nonstop hustle might reward a few high performers but will quietly alienate employees whose priorities also include caregiving, creativity, or community engagement. Alignment is about creating a culture flexible enough to integrate the realities people already live in while maintaining a cultural model that serves the mission of the company.

Types of Organizational Culture

In organizational psychology, organizations are frequently divided into one of four categories based on the organization's values, purpose, and mode of operating. As with any model, even an organization that can fit well within one category will at times deviate from the norm in one or more ways, and it is possible and even common for an organization to have qualities from more than one category. Furthermore, just as operations often shift over time, so do categories. Changes in organizational structure can be intentional, due to new company ownership or leadership, or the organization can operate as a hybrid of more than one model. Still, although these categories are not infallible, they offer a useful framework for understanding the values and priorities of organizations.

Clan Culture

This is the "family business" category. Members of a clan culture take one another's positions into account before making decisions. They often describe themselves as "close-knit" or "like a family," even when they aren't literally comprised of blood relatives. As a company scales larger, it is difficult to stay committed to this type of culture; however, that doesn't mean qualities of it won't show up even in a company that has gone from just a few employees to dozens or more. One positive quality of clan culture is collaborative decision-making, as these organizations often seek feedback from every employee at an organization, no matter how low-level their position may be.

However, this is a culture that comes with a high risk of boundary blurring, particularly when it comes to emotional boundaries.

Hierarchical Culture

When someone is asked to describe how a business operates, their mind often cuts straight to a hierarchical organization. It is the most traditional and common type of business structure. When an organization operates according to hierarchy, there is a strict chain of command, clear policies, and deference given to leaders for decision-making. At the top there are the executives, then managers of different departments, and onwards down. At every level, managers have direct reports, and the org chart dictates who is accountable to whom; any concerns that need to be addressed to top-level leadership will surface through the lower leadership ranks. When accountability operates as it should, the gears keep turning smoothly. If accountability breaks down at any point in the chain, cultural misalignment occurs and performance suffers.

Adhocracy

For adhocracies, the constraints on decision making are looser, and they're less likely to conform to a rulebook or strict chain of command. Many startups qualify as adhocracies, encouraging agile decision making and risk-taking. In dynamic industries like finance or tech, employees must be able to think on their feet and ask forgiveness rather than permission. Creativity and innovation are rewarded the most, and the ideal expectation is that big risks yield big rewards. It's tough to get involved in a company like this at an entry level—newbies are expected to step into their role and start running right away. Other organizational models often take on the characteristics of adhocracies, sometimes intentionally and sometimes accidentally.

Market-Driven Culture

Organizational cultures that are market-driven are the most focused on the bottom line. External factors such as demand, ROI, and billable solutions guide the choices they make. As in adhocracies, agile decision-making is important, but competition is also strongly emphasized. At every turn, employees and leadership ask themselves what they can do to make more sales, what the market itself is looking for, and how the company can market itself to achieve its sales goals.

Organizations and Accountability

For any of these organizations, accountability is essential. Hierarchical culture has methods of accountability built in: everyone has a supervisor to whom they're accountable, and any problems that arise are dealt with by distinct rungs of the ladder. People perform better when they're being watched and know that someone is holding them to due dates and other performance standards.

With other organizational culture models, accountability may be more nebulous. In an organization that is primarily an adhocracy, there may not be time to run decisions by someone higher up. The priority is to make a decision, and employees are less likely to be penalized for acting on their own—in fact, they may even receive more support from the higher-ups for bypassing the chain of command if the decision pays off.

Since adhocracies often emerge organically, as businesses scale, there are more opportunities for misalignment within this model. Roles and responsibilities can become more freeform, which may result in blurred boundaries and confusion about what an employee should be doing (we'll get into more detail about clarifying job roles in the next chapter). Behavioral expectations and values might not be communicated to new employees, and organizations end up with problems like office managers who provide poor customer service or a sales department that makes the bare minimum number of calls each day.

Leaders need to frequently revisit stated organizational culture and make sure they align from the C-Suite to the customer service department. Everyone should receive periodic reminders of values, be able to easily access company policies (such as in a print or digital handbook), and take time as needed to revisit job descriptions to make sure people understand the role they're expected to perform.

Organizations and Adaptability

Because of the naturally shifting nature of organizational culture, leaders need to know when to be adaptable and when to stand by existing values. When hiring, either permanent employees, contractors, or consultants, it must be clear how the organization sustains itself. Keeping in mind the four types of organizations can be helpful when trying to recognize points of friction and avoid misalignments.

One case I observed was with a newly appointed president of a retail company. The company's market position was in direct competition with similar companies, and therefore the organization's focus was heavy on sales and marketing. The president had recently hired a consultant who suggested they phrase emails with less emphasis on competition. The president pushed back, saying that as a market-driven company, competition was a core value of their organizational culture. After a few frustrating weeks, the continued misalignment meant the consultant's engagement cost a lot of money but went nowhere.

While some values cannot or should not be changed, an adaptable organization has a clear edge in the market. The concept of "strategic agility" has become a defining factor of long-term success, and today's leading companies empower teams to respond in real time to customer needs, market trends, and internal challenges. Netflix pivoted to streaming after years of mail-in DVD rentals. Slack marketed itself as a video game platform before realizing its ideal placement was as a professional communication tool.

But organizations themselves don't adapt—people do. In cases where your culture needs to adapt to a changing world, leaders should focus on holding onto their values while shifting strategies. While methods of accountability and core values need to be shared by everyone at the organization, a healthy culture rewards experimentation and treats failures as learning tools.

Adaptability is also key when creating an environment that prioritizes employee wellbeing and performance. Purpose and values can stay the same, but flexibility can help employees feel valued too. Policies that enhance wellbeing can be shaped to accommodate employees with differing needs, and employees can become more engaged with the work itself because they've been empowered to make their own decisions.

Use Case: Caregiving and Hybrid Work

On the whole, organizations have had to be adaptable to one major change in our greater culture that expands past the confines of the physical and digital office: a growing number of employees are also caregivers.

Caregiving is no longer something that people do when they're off the clock. According to recent studies, over 60% of U.S. employees report having caregiving responsibilities, either for their children, their aging parents, or for members of the "sandwich generation," both at the same time. Currently, the majority of these caregivers are women, but men are increasingly adopting caregiving roles as well. Regardless of gender, someone who is juggling work with raising children, supporting aging parents, or caring for a loved one with chronic illness carries responsibilities that don't disappear when the workday starts.

This means that the delicate dance of balancing caregiving and work roles affects more than just a few employees at a given organization—it's often the norm. Most Americans are juggling two or more full-time roles: their work role and their caregiver role among many others. Yet, the traditional 9-to-5 work structure was not built with caregiving in mind, and with "always on" culture on the rise, the risk of pre-burnout in these employees is much higher. Caregivers often face both rigid expectations and unpredictable demands, all with a lack of support; it puts them on a fast track to burnout. If organizations don't adapt, morale can plummet. These conditions often reinforce inequities that disproportionately impact women, people of color, and low-income workers.

To be truly effective, caregiver support must be embedded into the organizational culture—embraced by leadership, modeled by managers, and normalized across the workforce. To be able to apply those principles, leaders must know the type of organization they actually are and then adapt accordingly.

Employee wellbeing, and the policies that encourage it, can serve as an easy entry into understanding how cultures chafe against the needs of individual employees. Addressing the intersection of caregiving and hybrid work is a great example of how organizations can adapt to the nature of work in the 2020s. Organizations that have successfully created friendlier environments for caregivers have implemented key policies and programs:

- **Flexible Work Arrangements:** Options such as flexible start/end times, compressed workweeks, and asynchronous schedules allow caregivers to manage both work and home responsibilities without sacrificing performance.
- **Remote and Hybrid Work:** Even part-time remote work can make a meaningful difference by reducing commute time and allowing employees to be physically present for caregiving needs.
- **Paid Caregiver Leave:** Separate from vacation or sick leave, this provides dedicated time for employees to attend to medical appointments, caregiving transitions, or recovery periods.
- **Backup or Emergency Care:** Some employers partner with third-party services that provide emergency child or elder care, offering a safety net when usual arrangements fall through.
- **Employee Resource Groups (ERGs)**: Caregiver-focused ERGs offer peer support,

practical resources, and community. When well-led and properly supported, these groups reduce isolation and create visibility for caregiver concerns.

These supports can significantly reduce stress, increase job satisfaction, and help retain top talent, but only if leaders demonstrate and encourage their use. Policies don't live on paper—they live in practice. Leaders need to be adaptable and do the work needed to encourage the company culture they want to see.

Reinforce Values by Walking the Talk

Frequently, the values written on a company website are lofty. "We value good communication and lifelong learning" sounds noble and makes good website copy. The less approachable the policies are, the more you can bet they are more performative than operational. What has the company done to actually implement "lifelong learning"? If nobody can answer this question, it's time to take stock of where organizations can find practical applications to make their values real or re-evaluate their values altogether.

Policy changes, such as those around hybrid work or forms of accountability, might be advertised on the company website as a boon for employee flexibility or the mythical "work-life balance." All the while, in actual practice, leaders model workaholism and pressure others to follow. A new paradigm for decision-making, such as changing from a top-down approach to a collective one, might be pointless if higher-ups use their positions to influence employees one way or another. Just having new rules isn't the same as upholding values. If they are not incorporated into the structure of daily operations, who's going to remember any of it?

While many are convinced that cultural initiatives simply don't work, there is evidence that they can. The same study that reported how 72% of cultural initiatives failed *also* discovered that employee trust scores did rise to 26% at companies where cultural initiatives succeeded.[2] Branded campaigns and catchy slogans weren't necessary in any of these successful cases. The transformation came once leadership evaluated its own behavior and genuinely changed the way they led. They embodied the culture shift rather than plastering it all over the place like wallpaper.

Bringing an organization into alignment with its stated values means taking stock of the culture you have and the culture you want to have, then implementing new ways of operating that nudge you toward that goal. For a more market-driven organization, encouraging good-natured competition and implementing incentives for high sales might bring people into alignment with a culture that values revenue growth. For a clan culture, it may mean asking for feedback from the people at lower levels in the company and demonstrating how their comments are being applied to the organization. Leaders can change their company cultures in observable ways.

- **Leadership Modeling:** When leaders talk openly about subjects like caregiving and inclusion, encourage employees to get involved in events designed to support culture initiatives, and show their commitment to living company values in their decision-making, employees will

---

2. Ibid.

come to believe that cultural change goes beyond words.

- **Manager Training:** Managers are more tuned in to employees' day-to-day work, and managerial behavior often makes or breaks employees' belief in company culture. Of everyone at the organization, managers need to be trained to make their buy-in to values clear.
- **Open Dialogue:** Research has shown that 69% of employees regularly withhold feedback, fearing either retaliation or that they won't be listened to at all. Creating safe, encouraging environments for employees to give feedback is essential.[3]
- **Accountability and Metrics:** Organizations should collect data in more areas than just performance metrics. They should also track participation in benefit programs, group initiatives, and any other indicators of cultural change.

People are the primary strategic assets in any organization, and most of them respect consistency. Commitment to cultural changes that promote alignment between the organization's values and employees' experiences is a key part of helping employees establish life balance and enthusiasm about their work. An organization's values should be clear just from the way leaders of the organization behave. If employees have already bought into the company values as they understand them, they'll be less likely to burn out. Remember: It's not just about accommodations—it's about

---

3. Ibid.

putting the full weight of your organization behind making systemic change.

4

Embracing Role Clarity and Protecting Boundaries

In a best-case scenario, potential new hires at an organization read a job posting with an accurate title and description and enthusiastically apply, knowing that they fulfill the requirements for education, skills, and job history, and because they see the company as aligning with their values in key ways. When they start work, their role includes responsibilities that match the job posting, and they walk into work with a clear picture of what is expected from them.

Unfortunately, this best-case scenario isn't the norm.

Sometimes a person's actual work bears little resemblance to their job description. In reality, many smaller organizations hire only when current employees are overburdened with work. They want to offload tasks to someone else, but they don't have an organized plan. These cases force new hires to guess at what is expected of them, using only their titles, handbooks (which may or may not be up to date), and the whims of their higher-ups.

"What am I supposed to do as an 'office manager'?" an

employee with a vague job description might say. "Do I answer the phones? Am I in charge of checking the general inbox? Do I also…" and on and on.

As a company grows, things only get more confusing. The employee who already has a tenuous grasp on what they should be doing now splits responsibilities with another person. They have an endless list of things that need to be done, and while one person may take it upon themselves to do as much as possible, others are then left with busywork well below their pay grade. Blurred boundaries between your role and the role of other employees creates an unstable situation, which leads to resentment, toxic work environments, and eventually, employee burnout.

So far, we've looked at two types of boundaries: physical ones, like separating your home office from family space, and emotional ones, like resisting an 'always-on' culture that keeps employees tethered to their phones. The third type is just as critical: boundaries that separate responsibilities according to organizational role.

In many professional and personal contexts, roles are understood as increasingly fluid. At work, employees might be asked to "step in" or "wear multiple hats" without clear handoffs or accountability. At home, one partner might take on multiple tasks—nurturing, educating, cleaning, and cooking, for example—without receiving any support. Boundaries around roles identify who is doing what, and one of the best ways to prevent burnout is to make those boundaries as clear as possible both at work and elsewhere. Expectations should be well defined while maintaining boundary permeability. There are always times when people must take on additional or different roles than what they are used to, but the end goal is for an employee to have the autonomy to protect their own boundaries and adaptability to temporarily take on additional roles if required.

How Undefined Roles Lead to Burnout

Many work-related causes of burnout can be precipitated by unclear boundaries between roles and responsibilities.

- Having little or no control over work priorities
- Lack of recognition or reward for good work
- Unclear or overly demanding job expectations
- Chaotic or high-pressure environment

Imagine this all-too-common scenario: The team begins their workday with a surprise—their department supervisor says they need a report on their desk by the end of the next day. This report has not been assigned to anyone in particular, and the team is left on their own to sort out who does what.

Chaos follows. One person digs through the shared drive, unsure which version of the data is current. Another, wracked with guilt, takes on most of the work alone and dismisses a teammate to busy work. A third decides the report isn't their responsibility and checks out entirely. The next day, an absent coworker strolls in already holding the finished report. The scramble was for nothing.

In this type of environment, employees may worry they're asking the wrong people for help or looking to the wrong authority figures. They may be unsure whether they're prioritizing the right tasks, and they may fear being chastised by a supervisor no matter what choice they make. In chaotic workplaces, validation and recognition fall by the wayside. Employees often feel like they're failing at everything—even though many of them are actually doing a reasonably good job with the huge number of tasks they've taken on.

Living with this daily self-doubt perpetuates a culture of burnout. Some employees are strained because their disorderly environment overwhelms them. Others feel undervalued and lose sight of why they joined the organization in the first place. The individual harm depends on multiple factors, such as employees' personalities, the variety of roles they play in their day-to-day lives, the supervisor's openness to feedback and acting on it, or even the physical or virtual space they use for team meetings, which could be causing increased friction between team members. Whatever the personal reasons or situations, cases like these make people feel inadequate and cynical, causing their overall quality of life to plummet.

Shared Credit and Invisible Labor

When responsibilities aren't clearly defined or regularly revisited, they often fall unevenly. Certain personalities are especially prone to overcommitting, while other employees are left with less to do. While you may get a few people here or there who are happy to slack off, most people hate being underutilized at work. It leads to them feeling useless and fearing for the future of their jobs.

In my academic research, I observed the different roles parents play and the effect those roles have on their wellbeing. Parents have overlapping identities that they have to balance every day: driving kids to school, volunteering for extracurricular activities, and caring for children when they are sick. All of these roles are interconnected and overlapping, and parents don't just switch off their sense of responsibility when they clock in for work. Just as the roles of a parent are multifaceted, so too are the roles of a person at work. They may be a supervisor to some, but a subordinate to someone else. They may be a team leader in one group, while playing the role of a silent member in another team.

I have found that, to their own detriment, primary caregivers are the people most likely to step in and "just get it done." Caregivers are typically more empathetic and more willing to step up, both at home and in organizations. More often than not, these caregivers are women who have often been socialized to volunteer quickly and pick up the slack for others. Meanwhile, a lower-level employee who sees their position as "just a job" is left with little to do. Left with only simple or monotonous tasks, employees don't feel adequately challenged at work, leading to apathy, which is a major contributor to high turnover rates. Not only does this create major inefficiencies, it also leads to job insecurity for the employees still at the company.

This whole situation is a common example of how resentment builds up between team members. The people who are used to taking on extra work resent that, once again, they are doing everything themselves. The others resent the go-getter in return, and *everyone* resents their manager for putting them in this uncertain position. Rinse and repeat, and the negative feedback loop rolls on.

Organizational cultures that do not prioritize balance also do not reward those who are prone to taking on too much responsibility. Rather, the credit is often given to the team or the department as a whole. If there aren't clear boundaries between roles, some who are already busy may feel pressured to work themselves into the ground for the good of the department or the company. Ironically, caregivers who "wear many hats" can struggle most when their role expectations are not clear. Societal expectations and available support are always a moving target for the caregiver employee, even if they're giving one hundred percent of their energy to both their parental and employee roles.

Competing Values and Glorifying Multitasking

People often juggle multiple roles within each domain of their life (home life, work life, social life, and others). The same role confusion that plagues workplaces often shows up at home. Parents juggle the roles of caregiver, teacher, nurturer, protector, and even learner—sometimes all in the same hour. At times, it is hard for parents to shift their energy from one role to another. Without support, they may also find themselves spending more time in one role than the others. When parental roles seem imbalanced in some way, parents feel the same strain employees do at work: overwhelmed, undervalued, and stretched too thin.

This pressure to do it all poses unique issues, especially when people are working from home. The way people behave in the workplace does not always align with the way they behave with their families, and the growth of hybrid work increasingly complicates those divisions. Individuals apply different value sets to their work and personal lives, and these competing values often inhabit the same space and time slots when they work from home. If parents are multitasking at work and at home all at once, they may find themselves in roles that they wouldn't want to model to their kids.

As they hop from one domain to another, making coffee, taking phone calls, stealing moments away from the computer to spend time with their kids, they behave in different, sometimes conflicting ways. For some, switching roles is easy, but others may find themselves in work roles at home or home roles at work. While difficulty switching between roles doesn't by itself create the problems, when combined with the blurred boundaries between work roles and home roles, caregiving employees find themselves in a unique situation where that rubber band doesn't get a chance to rest or return to its original form. It remains stretched, threatening to snap at any moment.

Competing values can show up when a parent in a high-pressure role working from home might need to behave more aggressively in certain scenarios. This sort of behavior could be the opposite of how they want their kids to see them. Grappling with clashing values could lead to employees reevaluating their career choices. Other times, people do want their kids to see them in money-making mode, whatever that may look like. In such cases, personal values don't conflict with the values they prioritize in their job.

Either way, it's essential that caregivers have the autonomy to protect the boundaries between work and other areas of their lives as they see fit. When one is unsure of what they should be doing and when, that balance becomes harder if not impossible to achieve. The lessons they teach their children clash with the way they behave in their jobs. If an organization claims to support caregivers, they will create clear boundaries for roles and responsibilities, so everyone knows how and where they can be flexible.

Encouraging Accountability in Every Type of Organization

While smaller organizations may see it as unnecessary, or even overly rigid, clarity of expectations is at the heart of any healthy organization. If it isn't present, as the organization grows, cracks become more obvious and problematic. At one company where I consulted, the leadership team and I learned this firsthand.

"What do each of the employees in this department do?" I asked the CEO at the beginning of our engagement. He looked like he'd been suddenly caught in a spotlight, clearly at a loss. He said, "Well, this is the billing department."

"Do you have an org chart?" I asked, trying a different angle. "Role descriptions for you and your team members?"

The answer was no; he had nothing to help me understand who did what within his organization. It was a company of almost thirty people, and not a single role description had been written. While in the grand scheme of things, thirty is not a huge number of employees, it is more than enough employees to create major issues when roles are poorly defined, and accountability chains shift by the day.

As we reviewed in Chapter 3, the four organizational cultures—clan, adhocracy, hierarchy, and market—handle accountability very differently. Some naturally support clear roles and responsibilities; others lean toward ambiguity that can slow progress. As a result, some cultures are more suited to include clear roles and accountability. For instance, organizations may take on qualities of an adhocracy over time, regardless of how the organization began. While this can theoretically make businesses more agile, it can also slow progress to a creep. This is because a lack of accountability leaves employees confused about what they should be doing and blaming each other when things don't get done.

The CEO I mentioned earlier was running a business

based on clan culture. Especially in the early stages, these organizations often use a democratic approach to decision-making. Everyone gets a say in what happens moving forward, and responsibilities are assigned through consensus. While this may work early on, as these companies grow, continuing with clan culture creates major issues—eventually, managing the organization is like trying to control a boulder rolling downhill. Hires are expected to jump in and start running because there is no structure to ease them in. To maintain a coherent clan culture, roles need to be well-defined. It's also essential to regularly check that people at all levels of the organization are working on the right things in order to stay on track.

While leaders of clan, adhocracy, and market-driven cultures may not think they need a hierarchical structure, each of these culture types can benefit from exploring the components of hierarchical models, allowing them to pick and choose what might work for them. Leaders can take inventory of what needs to be done at their companies and create a system for how tasks are assigned within their teams. This can be done in any organization, including ones where people are expected to "go with the flow" more often than they would at a major corporation. However, hierarchical cultures are not off the hook—a hierarchical culture does not, by itself, make expectations clear. Boundaries can blur within any type of organizational culture.

Consequences of Poor Accountability

Roles and responsibilities should be clearly defined, but organizations also need systems to ensure people actually follow them. Even with structures and workflows in place, it's common for employees to drift outside their roles or neglect core responsibilities. If there is a volunteer role, the slackers tend to make themselves invisible, and the already burdened employee takes on additional roles for the good of the company.

I worked with one CEO to identify what was causing his company to lose money. The company was operating with a hierarchical culture where the chain of command, and therefore communication, was typically linear. Employees report to their managers, who report to their department heads, and up to the executives. To diagnose the problem, we needed to look at what was happening at every level rather than just taking the word of his direct reports.

We determined there was a missing link in the chain. Communication was breaking down because of one department manager. (I'll call him Brent.) From the outside, Brent appeared to be a very busy, very conscientious boss—he was always cleaning up messes and picking up the slack. Following the hierarchical chain of command, he'd bring grievances from his direct reports to the rest of the company. His department was underperforming, and he claimed it was because team members didn't feel supported by the rest of the organization.

This department manager believed he was holding the department together by taking on additional responsibilities. In reality, as distorted communication flowed upward and downward, everything became filtered through his personal preferences, and so he became a bottleneck. What Brent saw as saving the team was actually undermining it.

When an organization starts losing money or dealing with internal difficulties, it's time to break out the org chart and job descriptions. There should be a head of every department and known direct reports to that department. Each role should come with a set of Key Performance Indicators (KPIs) that determine success. With one of my clients, we implemented skip-level meetings, where a member of the leadership team skips their immediate subordinate (the department manager) and meets directly with team members instead. This creates an added layer of accountability no matter what your organization's culture may be. If employees at each level of the organization know what they're accountable for and who they are accountable to, this will go a long way to help leadership identify where pain points are when something isn't right.

Boundaries Make Organizations More Adaptable

Individual wellbeing is essential to the health of an organization. It may seem counterintuitive, but the better an organization becomes at drawing boundaries between roles and providing employees with autonomy to protect their own boundaries, the more adaptable they can stay in the market. Boundaries and adaptability can co-exist with each other. In fact, when each member's unique value is emphasized by defining their responsibilities, employees respect one another more and feel more secure in their jobs. Leaders get clearer pictures of how to delegate work, who should implement and execute new strategies, and who to hold accountable for the work. Leadership and employees alike spend less time and energy scrambling to figure out what exactly is going on.

In this way, boundaries can help individuals grow within their positions rather than constrain them. In fact, without boundaries, it is much harder to recognize growth opportunities. Anyone who has ever developed a skill will tell you that growth comes from pushing just beyond your boundaries. Clear boundaries don't box employees in— they make growth *visible*. With well-defined roles, it's easy to see when someone is stretching into new skills versus just drowning in unspoken expectations. Without that clarity, what looks like growth may just be silent exhaustion.

For boundaries to be effective, they must be reinforced with accountability. Clear expectations reduce confusion and suspicion, while helping employees distinguish between their roles at work, at home, and in the community. This clarity makes it easier to focus on priorities and manage the many hats they wear.

When boundary protection is a cultural value, it also becomes easier to support people's roles outside the organization. For example, if an employee has childcare responsibilities that fall at the same time as the weekly team meeting, people may see them come late to every meeting and automatically judge them as "not pulling their weight" around the office. The employee shouldn't have to give up caregiving to make a standing meeting. In this instance the fix is simple: shift the meeting by fifteen or thirty minutes, all schedules permitting. That small change honors the employee's dual roles and allows them to show up fully for both work and at home.

Additionally, learning about boundaries around roles and responsibilities can help leaders intervene when employees show signs of pre-burnout or when they are going through a tough time in their personal lives. If their job role is clear, the leader can clearly communicate with other employees exactly how to be helpful. Tasks can be clearly delegated to members of the team with greater capacity at the moment. Instead of offering vague gestures like, "Let me know how I can help," colleagues can identify concrete ways to support the employee.

When physical and emotional boundaries are valued—as well as boundaries between roles and responsibilities—employees have an easier time protecting those boundaries.

Protected boundaries around roles promote clarity, reduce reactivity, and help teams collaborate more effectively. They also encourage harmony within an organization and make it agile and self-aware enough to pivot whenever the market calls for it.

5

Microcultures and the Corner of Discontent

In the previous chapter, I introduced you to Brent, the crimp in the communication pipeline between his department and his organization's executive leadership. His story highlights the importance of accountability, but it also reflects something else that's key to understanding organizational misalignments: the power of microcultures.

Microcultures are small, distinct cultural groups that exist within a larger society, whether at work, home, or in the community. They develop around shared values, behaviors, interests, or roles. Examples include:

- A workplace department (e.g., Marketing or IT)
- An Employee Resource Group (ERG) at work
- A parenting group or school PTA
- A religious or spiritual community
- A group of friends that shares specific interests or ideologies

Each microculture has its own customs and dialects. While one microculture might encourage vulnerability and open dialogue (e.g., a women's leadership ERG), another might reward competitiveness and assertiveness (e.g., a sales team). Even moving between two "healthy" microcultures requires effort, and the emotional and cognitive demands of this code-switching impact an employee's well-being more than many leaders realize. Just as importantly, the values upheld by a microculture—whether explicit or unspoken—can either reinforce or quietly erode the organization's broader culture.

Because Brent was not being held accountable by his boss, executive leadership knew little about the microculture within his department until we investigated. It turned out he was running his own department in whatever way he saw fit, and whenever there was any pushback, the blame was passed on to leadership.

"Leadership is making me enforce this new policy," he would tell his team any time a decision seemed likely to be unpopular. "Personally, I think it's kind of dumb, but nobody asked me."

When he reported to leadership, his tune changed. "My team is the best at what they do!" he'd tell them. "They're exceeding expectations daily."

Customer complaints were piling up regarding Brent's team, but his boss dismissed them as outliers, taking Brent's word that all was well. She didn't recognize that Brent, and the microculture of mistrust he encouraged within his department, was the source of major cultural misalignment. Their microculture was ruled by the shared belief that executive leadership was out to get them, and that value brought everyone in the department together. Ironically, what bonded them internally was the very thing that isolated them from the rest of the company. Unfortunately, their perspective did not align with the company's stated values, which prioritized open communication and transparency. Like a harmful organism within a body, the department caused dysfunction in the rest of the organization.

Even within organizations whose employees number in the single digits, microcultures will always exist. They are neither inherently good nor bad. They simply exist, and whether they strengthen or destabilize the organization as a whole depends on how well their internal values align with the larger system. While leadership often attempts to affect culture from the top down, overlooking the everyday reality of microcultures almost guarantees misalignment. Working with microcultures directly is essential to bringing the entire organization's values into practice.

The Origins of Microcultures

Microcultures don't develop in isolation—they grow within the larger culture of an organization. They evolve as people come and go and as relationships shift. For instance, someone returning from maternity leave might find that the group now communicates in new ways. A new hire, while adapting to the existing microculture, also changes it simply by being there. Policies, departmental restructures, and leadership changes further reshape how a microculture looks and feels. In this way, microcultures are both reactive and generative; they are shaped by circumstances even as they shape what comes next.

Microcultures should not be confused with subcultures. Subcultures are broader in scope and may last a lifetime, like an ethnic or religious group, while microcultures live within the subcultures of an organization. Much of what I've emphasized in this book is how one part of a person's life affects all the others. Even with boundaries in place, the different domains an individual passes through can't be completely separated from one another. In the same way, microcultures can't be neatly cordoned off; they are porous and influence one another constantly.

When concentric circles are laid on top of one another, all of them are enmeshed to the degree that any shift in one circle changes the nature of the others. Even a tiny shift in one circle could create an entirely different formation within the cluster. Microcultures can also be compared to microorganisms within the body. We don't think much about them on a day-to-day basis, but they can have major impacts on the way our systems function. And, like microorganisms, we only start to notice them when the larger system begins to fail. The danger is that by the time leadership pays attention, the imbalance is already spreading.

Most people underestimate the number of cultures they navigate in a single day. There may be a "corporate meeting room" culture in the morning, a "preschool drop-off line" culture at noon, and a "book club" culture in the evening. There can even be one culture when two departments meet and work together, and two others when they work separately. The roles people play in those different microcultures can often contradict each other. People can move between them unconsciously, rarely pausing to ask whether the shifts align with their values or simply wear them down.

But those contradictions take a real toll on energy and identity.

Sometimes when I speak on this topic, leaders assume that their goal should be to eliminate microcultures altogether. This is misguided, and it demonstrates a fundamental misunderstanding because people always function as people, regardless of whether they're at home, work, or elsewhere. Microcultures are not automatically negative, but are in fact part of what makes human life so rich. However, problems arise when people adopt them subconsciously and uncritically, automatically following the norms that surround us, even when those norms contradict the organization's (or even their own) values. Left unchecked, a microculture that seems harmless can quietly erode trust. Once the microculture becomes toxic, it harms individuals and, more often than not, the organization too.

How Toxic Microcultures Take Hold

At one organization where I consulted, I met an office manager named Debbie. Debbie was unhappy in her job because she believed it was a dead end with no room to progress. She was planning to quit soon, once she found a new job where she could advance her career. Even though she was close to burnout in her current role, Debbie saw a new open position at the same company as an opportunity to find new meaning and motivation at work, so she applied.

Like many good organizations would, they made sure to follow a carefully created hiring process to eliminate any potential biases, especially since they had several internal candidates apply. Management conducted two rounds of interviews, each involving multiple interviewers in the room taking detailed notes. For every candidate, the interviewers cycled through the same set of questions.

Debbie was the most qualified candidate by far, and being offered the job was enough to keep her working for the organization. Whereas before she thought she was stuck, she was now excited to go to work again. Management was confident they'd chosen the right person to step up.

However, it is not uncommon for a microculture to

become toxic when several current employees apply for the same new role (with higher salary and benefits). Let's illustrate this with an example. Say another person applied for the same role, I'll call her Michelle. Michelle was unqualified and did not interview as well, but when she wasn't chosen for the promotion, she began to spread toxicity. Along with seeming completely checked out from her work, she spread rumors among her office clique that Debbie was promoted due to favoritism and that the interviews were a sham.

Fortunately, this organization valued a culture of transparency. The notes they took during the interviews and all the evidence they collected in the hiring process supported the fact that Debbie was chosen based on merit. She was the most productive, she had all the necessary skills, and she gave the best answers to the interview questions. Her promotion was indicative of how the organizational culture centered growth and fairness. But evidence alone couldn't neutralize the power of perception. Once mistrust takes root, corrective facts rarely travel as quickly as intriguing stories.

Even though Debbie is thriving in her new role, the microculture around her remains toxic. The rumor of favoritism lingers, leaving her isolated, despite her clear qualifications and strong performance. What began as one employee's jealousy spread into a shared narrative, showing how quickly perception can outweigh fact. It's a reminder that microcultures often take shape less from objective truth than from the emotions people hold in common, an idea that becomes even more important when we look at the subtle ways misaligned microcultures operate.

The Subtlety of Misaligned Microcultures

Since executive leadership is often separated from the rest of the organization, they may not hear rumors like the one that arose when Debbie got promoted. The way leadership becomes aware of problems with microcultures is usually through signs of burnout in their employees, the "red flags" of misalignment. People quitting without obvious reasons is one sign that they have been enduring a toxic microculture and can no longer cope. Inaccurate reporting from multiple sources, or reports that conflict with data, like in Brent's case, are all signs that something is wrong with the culture. Sometimes the warning shows up as inconsistency: what people say in meetings doesn't match what shows up in the numbers, or employees appear cheerful on the surface while privately disengaging.

When leaders recognize the signs that something is amiss, it's time for investigation. This is often where I, or a consultant like me, will intervene and conduct interviews, surveys, and even small group meetings to explore what microcultures exist in the workplace. The goal is to discover whether the body of the organization is suffering due to the micro-organisms—the microcultures—within it. Even when a microculture is only made of four or five people, like in Michelle's case, its toxicity will frequently seep into the larger organization.

One major challenge with this "red flag" approach is that, at times, toxic microcultures can produce some good outcomes for the organization. A department can hit KPIs and check off sales quotas even when a toxic environment is developing in their microculture. This paradox can mask deeper issues: outward success creates the illusion of alignment, even as trust erodes internally. People continue working in positions where there's toxicity for a few reasons. On one level, they may simply need the money or benefits; on another, they may feel that, as long as they're achieving the outcomes they were hired to achieve, the toxic people around them shouldn't matter. While toxic microcultures lead to clear red flags in some employees, others "stick it out," often continuing to perform in their roles as best they can.

This is one major reason why, when negative microcultures don't show obvious signs like missed deadlines or poor deliverables, they can hide in plain sight. From the top, everything looks fine: upper management sees the numbers or hears reports that the department is hitting its goals. In reality, problems may be simmering beneath the surface. It often takes more subtle clues, such as high turnover or repeated complaints about a department (whether from employees to HR or from customers), before leaders recognize the issue and step in.

Once the microculture problem is identified, leadership's goal is to do everything possible to move the microculture into alignment with the company's values. The goal is to run a company that holds the same values down to the last person in the company, even knowing that some microcultures may be in opposition to the company's culture. Sometimes that's effective, and sometimes it's not.

In truth, there is no way to root out every single toxic person or way of thinking within an organization. That would require a level of thought-policing that would certainly make the situation worse. However, a full cleanse isn't necessary to reach leadership's primary goal either. The goal is to build a team of individuals who are comfortable and competent in their jobs, and who are able to adapt to inevitable cultural ups and downs. In a microculture that's generally aligned with the organization, individuals can be confident that, when the inevitable toxic fumes blow into their environment, the air will clear at some point. They can trust that alignment between company culture and their own values will settle back into place because it's secure enough to weather the turbulence.

In the example of Debbie's microculture, aligning with the values of growth and transparency would be a slow process. Taking steps to eliminate pushback can make things worse before they get better. If a department is restructured, employees may become bitter and ask, "Why do they get to stay and I don't?" However, unless leadership takes steps to address toxic microcultures, they'll continue to create a negative feedback loop. As long as those working within a toxic microculture are in survival mode, they can't align with the organization's culture of growth.

Legacy Norms vs. New Leadership: Culture Clashes Ignite

Microcultural misalignments aren't restricted to lower levels in an organization. They can go all the way to the top, with one executive leader's behavior affecting the microculture among an organization's leadership team, or between that leader and those they supervise. Examples of these misalignments often occur when a new leader first starts working at an organization. It's common in large companies to use transitional periods to promote or hire more than one new leader, and the changes often upset the company's existing microcultures to a troubling degree. These transitions are especially vulnerable because legacy norms—the habits and values that have worked for years—collide with a leader's desire to prove themselves quickly.

Not long after one large retail company installed a new

president, they also hired a new sales director. She was brought in from outside the company to "fix their culture." However, some things within the existing culture were already working well. Ironically, this new hire identified those well-functioning parts of their microculture as the things that needed to be eliminated first. She wanted them to completely start from scratch, mistaking alignment with weakness rather than recognizing it as a strength.

The sales director was determined to change the department's market-based organizational culture into a hierarchical culture. She argued that creating a stratified org chart "lit a fire under employees and team members to do what they need to do." As it was, the only hierarchy present was a team leader and teams grouped by different products. The department thrived within this framework because employees were motivated by results, not structure.

The company president complained to me that this sales director didn't take the time to understand their company's culture before starting to implement changes. She came in with a fixed idea of how things could be done and started forcing its implementation without considering what might already be working. This caused strain both between her and the president, as well as between her and everyone working in her department. As a result, the sales team experienced decreased productivity, fell short of their targets, and started drifting toward a state of burnout. What she saw as decisive leadership was, in reality, creating a breakdown of trust.

When done right, aligning a microculture to the greater company culture is a slower process than most leaders would like it to be. Seismic changes always shift microcultures, but often at a higher cost than if those changes are made slowly. It can result in anything from individuals burning out and leaving to drops in a department's performance. However, if leaders take the time to learn about the successes and pain points within a microculture, they can harness what they learn to bring about the outcomes they want. Alignment, in other words, grows from listening first and acting second.

Realign Values by Meeting Microcultures Where They Are

In order to nudge microcultures in line with the organization's values, communication must be proactive, not reactive. When different people come together, microcultures arise organically as a result of different personalities bouncing off each other. Everyone has ingrained behaviors based on the environments in which they grew up. Much like how one person cooks rice in the rice cooker because that's how their grandmother did it, while another steams it on the stovetop for the same reason. Different customs and points of view, when brought together, will create unique microcultures that shift and change organically. These shifts aren't inherently bad; they simply reveal that people bring their whole histories with them to work, whether leaders acknowledge it or not.

Intervening against toxic microcultures is less a question of making everyone conform to the culture a leader desires than it is about asking, "Is this effective or not?" Even negative emotions can lead one to do something that's really effective, as when guilt motivates someone to complete overdue tasks. In other words, the test isn't whether a microculture looks "positive" on the surface, but whether its behaviors align with the organization's stated values and produce sustainable outcomes.

By looking at the red flags within their organization, one company I worked with finally identified where their problem was: their scheduling department. It had high turnover and poor retention rates, customer calls were being dropped, and they weren't scheduling nearly as many sales calls as leadership wanted them to schedule. From the leadership's point of view, they should have been making as many calls as possible to bring in more revenue, but that wasn't happening.

At first, leadership suspected that no one was monitoring the department. However, the schedulers had to log into a system that recorded all their calls, so they were constantly watched. The truth was that the schedulers were simply not doing their jobs. Though calls were logged, no one was tracking volume or quotas, which meant they were only making five or six calls a day, whereas they should have been doing at least twenty. There were no defined quotas or goals in place, and the microculture of that department was lackadaisical. The workers would spend their day intermittently working, chatting with one another, and taking long lunches and coffee breaks while making the bare minimum of calls. Their only incentive was their salary, which they got regardless of the amount of work they did. What had developed was not active resistance, but apathy reinforced by unclear expectations and a supervisor who was having a hard time keeping his team accountable.

The supervisor was fed up, mostly because his own supervisor was getting pressure from upper management and leaning on him to make major changes. Considering the temperament of the department, it would not have been wise to come in and demand "higher numbers or else." Judging by the existing microculture, it was clear those employees would have revolted against leadership and begun to view them in an "us vs. them" light.

Eventually, the supervisor's solution was to use the

"negative" traits of the microculture to the organization's advantage. He decided to implement a market-driven culture based on incentives. He started a leaderboard to drum up some friendly competition among the schedulers, where at the end of each week, whoever made the most calls would get a perk such as a coffee gift card. The employees' microculture was perfectly suited to this solution because it reframed their camaraderie into playful motivation.

In spite of their numbers starting out so low, there was no need to throw the microculture out completely. Instead, working with the existing microculture, they added an aspect of friendly competition. Team members already got along, so their existing microcultural roles meant that the "play" of friendly competition was welcome. It felt like a natural outgrowth of the culture they'd built organically. By meeting the group where they already were, leadership transformed the department's results without breaking the underlying bonds that made the team cohesive.

Adaptable Companies Create Adaptable Microcultures

The key to coming up with solutions for poor performance doesn't come from an iron fist. It comes from noticing the nuances of a microculture and shifting the environment to meet the organization's ultimate goals. This is a feature of an adaptable organization, one that accepts the organizational culture as it actually is. Working to improve it is nearly always more effective than imposing change from above without understanding the culture that already exists.

If a microculture thrives with a sales or market-driven culture, working within that framework will be much more effective than trying to overhaul it into a hierarchical culture. If a microculture is tight-knit and clan-like, asking them to become cutthroat is like carrying a heavy weight uphill when you could just take a streetcar instead. The misstep many leaders make is assuming that what motivates them as leaders will motivate their employees, too,which is why it's so important to bring a spirit of humility to see what already works before introducing something new.

Instead of forcing microcultures to conform, being adaptable and working with what's in front of you will keep morale higher and burnout rates lower. Professional outcomes are better when people feel comfortable within their microculture, because comfort creates the stability that allows people to stretch. Then, once they're closer to alignment with the rest of the organization, the people within those microcultures will be more adaptable, too.

6

The Human Cost of Cultural Misalignment

As human beings navigating the interconnectedness of ourselves, our communities, our workplaces, and our environment, we are hard-wired to think and act from a place of values. Individuals apply their own values in every domain of their lives, in every way that is relevant to that particular situation. Parents may value patience, kindness, and quality time with their kids and set standards for the way they interact with them according to those values. Someone who participates in community service may value civic responsibility. They may also value integrity and inclusiveness in a work context. Upholding personal values is more than just a tool that helps us exist in the world—it provides a way to live in alignment with our authentic selves.

An individual's personal values may vary, but each person constantly negotiates their own values with those imposed by the outside world (a classic example is new moms trying to live up to society's expectations). This is not necessarily harmful; it's a simple reality that society consists of people with diverse values. However, coordinating individual values with group values requires varying degrees of effort. Even under circumstances with low friction—where an individual's values generally coincide with the values of the group—moving through different spaces requires intentionality. Individuals must make multiple adjustments day-to-day, and often hour-by-hour.

I've highlighted how plentiful microcultures are across all domains. Behaviors, ways of speaking, and values are different even in groups that consist of fewer than five people. They also always overlap with larger cultures; individuals exist inside a microculture, while that microculture is nested within another, larger culture. The proliferation of microcultures means individuals must reckon with even more value nuances than simply those of their home, community, and their organizations.

Consider the microcultures one passes through over the course of a week and how they require adjustments in behavior. A cluster of cubicles at the office may have its own microculture that an employee participates in during working hours, while their usual lunch group has another. There can be one microculture when a parent spends time with their partner and children, and a different one when they bring their partner and children to spend time with the extended family. I once worked with a small company where the two teams that worked ten feet apart developed such different habits that employees joked about "crossing the border" when they walked from one to the other. That's how quickly and deeply microcultures take root.

Throughout our days, we're part of these small cultures within larger cultures—the microculture of the nuclear family within an extended family, the microculture of your department versus the greater company, the microculture of classroom volunteers within the greater culture of the school. When people must constantly adjust their behavior, their actions reflect the permeable nature of physical, emotional, and role-related boundaries. And if you've ever felt exhausted by those tiny shifts, you're not alone: this is the hidden cost of living in so many overlapping cultures.

Cognitive Dissonance Causes Burnout

Cultures of all sizes, both micro and macro, can chafe individuals in some areas more than others. Someone who values solitude negotiates that value with a need to communicate with coworkers and customers. For them, the daily culture of their workplace will cross their emotional boundaries more frequently than it will for others. A parent might value giving their kids freedom to say what they want, but that value may conflict with the standards of behavior their visiting grandparents might expect. Controlling the family's behavior blurs emotional boundaries, boundaries related to parental roles and responsibilities and, if the grandparents' visit happens to be at the parent's home, physical ones as well.

Adjusting one's behavior when they transition from one type of culture to another—often called "code-switching"—is mentally and emotionally demanding. Some cultures make people feel seen and give them the space to be more open about who they are and what they believe. Others require people to give up some of that self-actualization to fit in. The further one gets from their authentic self, the more effort is required to stay regulated and connected with their identity. Ideally, a person can function as closely to their true self as possible in every domain of their lives rather than bend themselves into countless different shapes throughout the day. When the environment keeps them from behaving according to their values, they become stressed, and if they face that pressure eight hours a day, Monday through Friday, the stress quickly becomes chronic.

Passing through so many microcultures day after day can take an emotional toll on a person, even in the most relaxed situations. At worst, an individual may feel as if they have no choice: either act against their values or lose their status (and in the case of organizational cultures, their job). Imagine an employee who prides themselves on patience and empathy working in a sales-driven department where the only thing that counts is speed. Day after day, they're rewarded for rushing through conversations—even when it cuts directly against the way they believe people should be treated. That constant push and pull creates a slow, grinding tension: they're outwardly performing well, but inwardly eroding.

When there is misalignment between an individual's values and the values of the microculture they're moving through, there is a greater risk of the individual starting to experience symptoms of pre-burnout. That risk stretches into the larger cultures too—if one of the individual's microcultures works against both their values and the larger culture's values, they will experience even greater distress.

Values misalignment creates cognitive dissonance in individuals. The angst that goes along with cognitive dissonance leads to poor outcomes in organizations, as we've explored in previous chapters. Sales numbers and other metrics drop along with employee morale and clarity. Some departments may have higher turnover rates, resulting in organizations having to invest more time and money in finding replacements. If you've ever wondered why a team with plenty of talent still can't seem to hold people, this is usually the culprit. The key to understanding these organizational issues lies in how misaligned values affect individual wellbeing—for both mental and physical health.

Individual Resilience Fails in the Face of Misaligned Values

If we return to an understanding of an individual employee as a rubber band, we can see the clear connection between value misalignment and burnout. Every time an employee is required to negotiate their values with those of their organizational culture, they stretch. That stretch creates tension within the individual. If their values don't contradict the organization's values, they don't have to stretch very far, and the rubber band can come back to a normal, relaxed state often and easily. However, if their values contradict organizational values, the individual is required to stretch further and for longer durations as they juggle opposing ways of behaving in different spaces.

If an employee is constantly stretched with no time to relax or realign with their true self, they're at risk of snapping, or reaching that state of burnout that often requires drastic measures to heal. If they are constantly under stress and stretched to their limits due to organizational misalignment, both the individual and the organization will suffer. Resilience doesn't mean being able to stretch forever. It means being able to recover. Without that chance to relax back into alignment, even the strongest bands eventually fray.

The Physical and Emotional Toll of Blurred Boundaries

In a world where boundaries criss-cross and balance is an ever-elusive concept, we need each of our spaces to align with who we are. Like the regular adjustments human beings make every day as they move between microcultures, even the best boundaries have some permeability. Even when a person draws boundaries for themselves, there will be both anticipated and unexpected circumstances that make it necessary to stretch, nudge, or even break through boundaries. Every time that happens, it applies pressure to the individual, and that affects the body.

This isn't an exaggeration. There is significant evidence that chronic, work-related stress can result in these physical and mental health symptoms:

- Fatigue
- Insomnia
- Sadness, anger, or irritability
- Alcohol or substance use
- Heart disease
- High blood pressure
- Type 2 diabetes
- Vulnerability to illnesses[1]

Blurred physical boundaries and overlapping spaces are a reality of a post-pandemic world; work enters home spaces via computers and devices. For some, sending "just

---

1. The Supportive Care, "How Chronic Stress Impacts the Immune System," *The Supportive Care* (blog), April 25, 2025. https://www.thesupportivecare.com/blog/how-chronic-stress-impacts-the-immune-system

one more email" at ten o'clock at night feels harmless. For an employee with a chronic illness, working from bed may be a necessary reality of remote work. But depending on an individual's values, transgressing physical boundaries might bump up against other priorities that require attention, like the ability to fully focus on relationships outside work. We've discussed how "always-on" culture also crosses physical boundaries. Having the workday bleed into unconventional hours may make it so someone neglects their value of a healthy sleep pattern or regular exercise. Anyone who's ever found themselves scrolling through emails on the sidelines of a kid's soccer game knows this tension firsthand: the body is present, but the mind is still at work.

Both the larger culture and individual microcultures at a company can also conflict with an employee's values. An employee may experience cognitive dissonance when their organization collaborates with a client whose point of view is out of step with their values. If they are opposed to doing work in a particular way, like using generative AI, they may feel emotional stress if the organization requires them to use it. Microcultures can further complicate this issue for employees, too. A toxic microculture of gossip or dishonesty may cause emotional stress in an employee who values transparency, and they may also feel conflicting loyalties to the microculture versus the overall organization's values.

A person's roles and responsibilities in an organization can also put them in situations where they either have to sideline their own values or make an effort to push back against whatever is causing their cognitive dissonance. If an employee values attention to detail and high-quality work, but their supervisor values speed at the expense of thoroughness, they will struggle to adapt. If a manager cares about letting employees rest and recharge, but the higher-ups require them to push direct reports to be more productive, they may start to feel negatively about themselves and their job. If an employee can't figure out what tasks they're supposed to accomplish, they may become fearful about getting scolded, or worse, fired. When employees have to wrestle with their values and boundaries on a daily basis, they feel helpless in their effort to create a sustainable, balanced life.

Cultural Misalignment Blocks Lifestyle Balance

Lifestyle balance is a concept that shifts along with periods of transition in an individual's life. The individual may need to prioritize family when their children are small, or they may need to prioritize their health and wellbeing when they are dealing with an illness. They may even go through periods of time where they're willing to put in extra time at work if their job requires it. If a person wants to avoid overwhelm and burnout, they need to continually allocate their limited energy to prioritize what matters most to them. I will discuss this in more detail in the next chapter.

Individuals have an easier time balancing their lives if the organization's culture is aligned with their values and leadership is respectful of employee boundaries. Organizational culture that blurs boundaries leaves employees uncertain of where they're supposed to put their energy and removes their autonomy to prioritize and plan. If an employee is glued to their work phone on a Saturday afternoon, even though they promised their full attention to their child's soccer game, they're prevented from aligning with their own parental values. If they have to say no to a community volunteer project because their supervisor hasn't clarified whether they'll be needed for an upcoming business trip, role confusion interferes with their commitment to their community. Both these cases demonstrate how, when an organization blurs boundaries and has unclear or inconsistent expectations, they interfere with an employee living a balanced, fulfilling life.

Consider this example of how unpredictable code-switching can cause unhealthy tension: If an individual is with their family at the park, they will probably be dressed in informal clothes and behave in a more natural, relaxed way. If they suddenly see someone from work, their entire demeanor may shift. Their body tenses; they stand up straighter, shift their tone, and quickly self-edit. That jarring moment is the recognition that they've left one micro-cultural "bubble" and entered another. It's such a small, ordinary moment, but anyone who's lived it knows how physically draining it feels. When individuals are constantly unsure of when they will have to switch into work-mode, they are more likely to hold that uncomfortable tension at all times, quite literally, in their physical bodies.

When an employee can't predict what an organization requires from them, there's also the risk of emotional exhaustion from constant code-switching. Like the rubber band, knowing that they may be called to change their behavior at any given moment stretches an employee and keeps them stretched for long periods of time. If they get the idea that they need to be "always-on" and are valued for their productivity and availability above all other things, they remain on a path that keeps them from being true to themselves. The draining and often disorienting side effects of having to flip from one way of being to another often end in burnout.

Employees are often adept at suppressing, negotiating, or abandoning their values to succeed, but organizations pay a price in retention, trust, and long-term sustainability. To avoid these pitfalls, organizations must clearly communicate their values and the boundaries their employees can come to expect. Then, organizations must operate in a way consistent with those values, so individuals can live sustainable lifestyles and remain satisfied with their jobs. While flexibility, both on the employee and the organization's part, will always be necessary to a degree, making expectations explicit lowers the level of cognitive dissonance that harms employee wellbeing.

Example: Employee Duties vs. Caregiving Responsibilities

For a common example of how misaligned values affect individuals, look no further than the challenges faced by employee caregivers and the organizations that employ them. From a 10,000-foot view, evidence shows that organizations that prioritize their employee caregivers are more adaptable to changes in the market. Those high-level successes only take place because of how leadership responds to individual employees.

At its most basic level, it benefits an organization to support caregivers, because when employee caregivers are not supported, they suffer. At the organizational level, failing to support employee-caregivers can result in:

- Burnout and Absenteeism: Unsupported caregivers are more likely to experience mental exhaustion, stress-related illnesses, and frequent absences.

- Turnover: Many employees—especially women—leave the workforce or step back from leadership roles when caregiving becomes incompatible with their job.
- Inequity: When only those without caregiving responsibilities can succeed, organizations unintentionally reinforce gender and class disparities.
- Loss of Talent: Experienced, loyal employees walk away, not because they want to, but because they can't afford not to.

In a real-world example, at a mid-sized technology company, the HR department noticed a spike in turnover among women in mid-career roles. A survey revealed that caregiving stress—especially post-pandemic—was a major factor in these women leaving the company. Providing them with ample formal caregiver leave, training managers to be empathetic and flexible with caregivers, and providing a caregiver ERG to connect them with community and support resulted in a twenty-five percent drop in turnover among caregiving employees, a measurable boost in engagement scores, and an increase in ERG participation across all demographics. The cultural tone shifted from silence to support.

Employee caregivers are becoming the norm across most organizations, and there are frequent areas where a caregiver's values conflict with the values and expectations of their workplace. A caregiver may want to be there for their kids, to help them with their homework or cheer for them at their soccer game, or they want to always be available if their child is sick. If a workplace's rules don't allow that type of flexibility, the caregiver is prevented from living up to those values. That results not only in guilt and angst for the caregiver, but it also means they are forced to find workarounds to make sure their children's needs are met in their absence, like muting a Zoom call to cover your kid coughing in the background, scrambling to find last-minute childcare when school closes, or rocking a baby to sleep with one hand while typing with the other. The trade-offs are impossible. When an organization forms and enforces its values around the needs of employee caregivers, it bears positive results for individual and organizational health and morale.

Positive results from consistent values benefit all employees, not just caregivers. Organizations that lead with empathy and flexibility see better retention, higher morale, and a more inclusive, resilient workforce. When accommodations are made for caregivers, they are better able to live within their own stated values. This is good news: flexibility for caregivers almost always ends up improving conditions for everyone else, too. The same goes for all employees who want to be able to give proper attention to the things they care about outside the workplace.

Why Organizational Values Must Be Both Clear and Embodied

For many leaders, directly connecting organizational culture and employee wellbeing is not intuitive. The organizational higher-ups often buy into an idea that the individual needs to be treated for burnout, instead of examining their own systems; essentially the impulse is to treat burnout like an individual flaw rather than a cultural signal. When I'm brought into an organization, leaders will often point to particular employees who are showing signs of burnout and say they need an intervention.

"I want to keep this person around," the CEO says to

me. "I'd hoped they would be my successor one day, but they seem really worn down, and I've heard rumors they're on the verge of quitting. You should probably focus on them first."

Unfortunately, improving this employee's wellbeing is not as simple as having 1:1 meetings with them. If nothing changes within the organization to meet the employee where they are, it may actually wear down the employee further by making demands on their time and energy. They have now received the message from leadership that they need to do better, but they don't feel any more empowered to make those changes than they did before the conversation.

When there is no cultural alignment, even well-meaning policies fall flat. Saying the right words isn't enough to encourage employees to be themselves. Imagine reading a glossy "we support parents" memo in the morning and then being told it's inappropriate to have pictures of your children on your desk. That contradiction destroys trust instantly. Following up words with actions builds trust.

An identity-eroding organizational culture asks employees to assimilate; that means hiding their personal beliefs or values, abandoning culturally significant practices, and suppressing their emotional authenticity, all to "fit in." If leaders don't want to pressure employees to assimilate, management needs to walk their talk. They should instead encourage acculturation, where employees can adapt to an organizational culture while still expressing their identities and making decisions according to their values. It's important to clearly state the organization's position, but organizations can only reap the cultural rewards if those positions are upheld through actions.

Focusing on building a healthy, values-aligned organizational culture creates better returns than chasing revenue. Clearly communicating values, and then living them, benefits the whole organization. Honoring an employee's need for lifestyle balance, rather than demanding they compartmentalize and put their job over everything else, helps them be more comfortable in the workplace. That comfort gives them room to innovate, complete tasks, make better decisions, and get along better with customers and coworkers.

Employees should experience psychological safety. When employees feel safe enough to be true to their values at work and know what is expected of them, they are likely to experience lower stress in other domains of their lives. They will be able to integrate their personalities, cultures, and personal ethos into the work they do, because they know where they stand in relation to their jobs. And when all those elements align, everybody wins.

7

Redefining Balance

It irks me to hear the term "work-life balance" used so frequently. The term makes it sound like work and life are two separate things, even though that idea directly contradicts the majority of people's lived experience. "Work-life balance" implies that work is not part of your life, or that you stop being a parent, spouse, community member, etc., when you enter your workplace either physically or virtually. The "balance" part of "work-life balance" makes it seem like it's possible to devote a perfect 50% of your time and energy to work and 50% to your "life," which apparently excludes your time spent at work.

That may work for an undercover CIA operative or a fictional character, but it's never been the case for me or anyone I've worked with. "Life" isn't a category that's separate from "work." "Life" isn't a useful umbrella term for everything that happens outside of the workplace. From day to day, people play many more roles than just employee and non-employee, and it's *never* a 50/50 split.

I prefer to use the more human-centered term: lifestyle balance. It does not imply that "work" is separate from "life," and it creates space for the shifting complexities each person faces as they try to fulfill their responsibilities without burning out. It makes space for the reality of human existence: everything in an individual's life—whether that be their job situation, their family life, their environment, their health, or one of the other myriad influences—is constantly changing.

Balance Isn't Static

You can never tell by looking at an individual's calendar alone whether their lives are balanced or not. When it comes to evaluating someone's lifestyle, "balanced" is not the same thing as "equal." Each individual's perception of a balanced life is subject to their energy levels, time, and priorities. But above all other factors, it's determined by their own perception of how satisfied they are with each area of their lives. Satisfaction levels are always fluctuating because so are our circumstances.

Consider what "balance" means for a person who is doing very well at work. She has just gotten a promotion, and her direct reports like and respect her. Company leadership is happy with her because her department started to bring in more revenue when she took over. Now, consider how you'd view that person's lifestyle balance knowing that she has no romantic partner, nor is she dating anyone. Should her life be considered unbalanced?

Unless we know her priorities and preferences, we simply cannot say. If this successful employee wants a romantic relationship, she will look at her situation and call it unbalanced. However, if she is in a period of her life where she is not interested in romance and is happy to stay focused on growing her career, she's not unbalanced at all. For this season of her life, even though she is emphasizing work more than relationships, she has lifestyle balance.

Lifestyle balance means different things to people in different roles at different times. Imagine you hear about a person who spends eight hours in the gym every week. Your first impulse may be to say that this person must do an amazing job balancing self-care with their other activities. Would you say the same thing if you were to find out this person was a professional athlete? Maybe, maybe not. But knowing that number doesn't help an outsider predict a person's lifestyle balance.

A person's season in life is a major consideration in lifestyle balance. A parent with a new baby will spend almost all their time devoted to the infant. To call a new parent on leave from work "unbalanced" for not devoting 50% of their time to work and 50% of their time to everything else is absurd. During this season of life, focusing completely on parenting and deriving satisfaction from that singular focus is a fully acceptable way to maintain lifestyle balance.

People start to feel out of balance when misalignments between their values and how they spend their time and energy start to crop up. Not coincidentally, that is often when people start creeping closer to burnout. Someone who is emotionally drained from working at a company that is misaligned with their values or working in a department with a toxic microculture that keeps them on high alert all day will feel dissatisfied with their work life no matter how much time they're spending on other parts of their lives.

Low satisfaction in one area of life often colors other areas of that person's life as well, because we don't become clean slates every time we move from one place to another. The boundaries in our lives can be so blurred—even at the best of times—that imbalance can lower satisfaction across the board. If an individual is having a hard time with their marriage, they carry negative feelings with them to the gym, to volunteering in the community, to work, and to wherever else they exist throughout the day. Managing lifestyle balance is an ongoing, evolving process. That's why it's important for people to periodically take stock of different areas of life to identify pain points and determine courses of action appropriate for that time and space.

Relational Models of Measuring Lifestyle Balance

The culminating work of my doctoral education explored parental decision-making and how parents balance the different roles required for them to raise their kids. The model I developed was originally meant for mothers, but I found that it applies to other caregivers, such as those caring for adults with autism, children with developmental disabilities, or the elderly. Many of these caregivers themselves have experienced mental health concerns, and the model has helped them discover ways to keep themselves balanced while still filling their most vital roles. I have successfully applied the model to leaders and employees of organizations. The remarkable thing is that the model can be applied to almost any population.

For the original population of mothers, roles cover the nuts and bolts of caregiving: driving kids to school, volunteering in the classroom, preparing snacks for extra-curricular activities, and the like. They also can be more esoteric and overlapping, like being a nurturer or a disciplinarian. These roles are all relational, meaning that they are all centered around the different identities a parent takes on to function as a parent. Once they listed out their roles, mothers would measure their satisfaction with their performance in each of them compared to how satisfied they wanted to be. The process helped them uncover where and how they could make changes that would prevent them from burning out.

During my research, I applied the Balance Mapping model to my own life and activities on several occasions. In one case, for my parenting model, I measured the following relational identities:

- Caregiver
- Nurturer
- Protector
- Educator
- Learner

Nurturing refers to activities that soothe a child, things like playing games, singing songs, cuddling, and reading stories. Instead of focusing on nurturing, I discovered I was leaning too hard into the "educator" role. I had become so rigid about my daughter following the rules that I'd all but forgotten about playtime or having fun with her. My daughter was behaving like she was irritated with me, and tension grew between us. At last, I realized she was upset with me because I was always barking orders at her. "Stop that!" or "Put that down!" or "No sugar before bedtime!" I was losing my focus on enjoying our time together. I would never have noticed the need to change if I hadn't analyzed my parenting by labeling and examining my actions within these different roles.

Once I had figured out what was going on, i.e., the fact that I had placed too much emphasis on "educator" and not enough on "nurturer," I was able to plot out actions to balance my parenting. First, I made a mini goal for myself to stop any time I was about to say something that was more on the educator/disciplinarian portion of the map. I developed a habit of considering whether what I was about to say absolutely *had* to be said at that moment, or if I could let it go. Most of the time, I didn't need to say what I was thinking. My daughter was a toddler with a short attention span; repeating the same things over and over to her wouldn't have made a difference.

When I realized everything didn't have to be a teaching moment, I was able to loosen up a little. It was okay if she occasionally had a sweet treat before bedtime, as long as she brushed her teeth afterward! My daughter was much more relaxed around me as a result, and it made my life as a parent much easier and more balanced as well.

To truly find balance, a person must align their energy, values, and attention with their actions in their current season of life. Understanding relational roles helps one identify their priorities and ways to act on them. And since everyone plays multiple roles in life, this exercise can help everyone, not just caregivers.

Balance Mapping and Its Applications

To measure and improve lifestyle balance, start by asking the question: "What are my roles in life, and how satisfied am I with them?" The Balance Mapping exercise asks individuals to do this, then compare two different states of being: current energy investment and level of satisfaction or fulfillment in that role. It helps them see not just where their time, energy, and resources are currently going, but also whether their current state matches their true desires. By reflecting on both current investment and satisfaction, those doing the activity gain clarity on where to make adjustments.

When I ask people to create their map for lifestyle

balance, the first step is to identify the roles they play. From there, the individual can chart how satisfied they are in their different roles, with a holistic view of how those roles influence each other. Potential roles a person might play throughout their lives include the following:

- Leader/boss
- Parent
- Caregiver
- Board member
- Mentor
- Friend
- Spouse
- Sibling
- Volunteer
- Community leader

To complete this exercise, start by identifying eight to ten different roles or domains of your life. The categories you choose should be your highest priorities.

- Each life domain (or key role) is plotted as a point on the map.
- Clusters in the **high resources, low fulfillment** zone may indicate pre-burnout or imbalance.
- The goal is to move more areas into **high resources, high fulfillment** (your zone of thriving).

[Figure 1: Balance Mapping Matrix]

Low Fulfillment
    High Fulfillment

High Resources

I put in extra hours at work, without recognition. I seem to be giving it my all, but I have a low level of satisfaction in my employee role.

I coach the local high school football team. We meet every weekend for practice and games. It is a lot of hard work, but the team is strong, and I feel a sense of pride when they win.

Low Resources

I don't have the time or money to join a gym or a yoga studio. I am

not fulfilled/satisfied by my physical fitness.

I sit on the board of a nonprofit whose mission is close to my heart. We only meet once a quarter, but I derive a sense of meaning and fulfilment in this role.

To download a copy of the Balance Mapping Matrix, visit https:// luminousconnections.net.

Remember, the plotted points will change over your lifetime with each season of life you are in. Quadrant selections by themselves do not mean your life is out of balance or that you're headed toward burnout; both of those states are subjective. There isn't a requirement that every area is in the right upper quadrant (high resources expended and high fulfilment achieved), and in fact, each area should *not* be in the same quadrant if you are being honest with yourself. This tool helps you identify ways to improve your life satisfaction, so a realistic view of where you currently are will only help you reach where you want to be more quickly.

If you are unhappy with the amount of time you spend in the gym, use the Balance Mapping exercise to figure out where you can make adjustments. If you could snap your fingers and create a new arrangement on your map, where would the new points land? Maybe you're prioritizing your social life in the evenings and are then too tired to wake up and go to the gym in the mornings like you had planned. Remember that we all have finite resources. There are still only twenty-four hours in a day and only seven days in a week. A shift in the time you spend in one area will automatically influence another area or areas. You may not need to completely shut down your social calendar, but if you really want to improve your satisfaction with your fitness, you can start with small changes, like committing to an earlier bedtime a couple of nights a week, thereby shifting your fitness satisfaction to a higher number, and time/energy you put into your social life to a lower number, all the while maintaining (or having a slightly diminished) satisfaction level with your social life. Balance Mapping gives you a visual tool to make adjustments in your lifestyle as situations change.

As I learned by applying the model to parenting, balancing different roles is a series of tradeoffs. For every additional role a person takes on, they are required to be adaptable. For you to devote energy to what will ultimately bring you greater overall satisfaction, you may have to give more to one area of your life by letting some things go in another. There might be a few more toys to pick up, and you may have to brush someone's teeth twice, but there will be fewer tears and tantrums. Balance means finding what works for you through executing small changes and being flexible throughout fluctuating circumstances.

Shifting and Overlapping Roles

Let's look at how different Balance Maps apply to someone over a longer period of time. In this simplified example, our subject, Nina, is balancing three different areas of her life: career, relationships, and caregiving, during different seasons. Throughout these seasons, her roles subtly adjust within these categories, and so do her levels of satisfaction.

In our example, Nina's first season is when she goes to university. At this point, her primary role is "student," and almost all of her energy is geared toward the "career" category. Nina has a girlfriend who is also primarily focused on school, and Nina's only caregiving responsibility is a betta fish. During this time, even if most of her energy is spent on studying, that doesn't make areas of lower responsibility unbalanced. However, as she enters a new season of life, her Balance Map changes.

Nina's satisfaction level for the "career" category takes a dive after graduation due to COVID tanking the job market, but then it rises again when she finally gets a job that makes her feel secure. Her "career" role has gone from student to unemployed person to employee. She performs well on the job for a while, but after a few years, leadership starts to notice her stagnating. Nina's managers start wondering what has changed at work that is making her behave so differently. What they don't realize is that the answer may be found outside of her employee role.

In the other two categories, relationships and caregiving, Nina's satisfaction levels have also been fluctuating. Around the time she was settling into her job, Nina got engaged and then married, her roles moving from girlfriend to fiancée to spouse. By her second year of marriage, her relationship with her spouse is at a low-satisfaction level, but she is in a holding pattern. She isn't happy in her spouse role, but she still has a high satisfaction level in her employee role.

Then, she and her spouse decide it's time to bring a baby into their lives, but Nina gives the condition that they need to deal with their relationship problems first. They start couples therapy to rehabilitate their marriage while simultaneously preparing for a baby. Around this time, while Nina is engrossed in improving her marriage and adding "parent" to her list of roles, her work stagnates. It is natural for people to refocus their values and priorities as their lives require, and no matter how badly someone may want to give 100% to every role, it's simply impossible. In fact, expecting that behavior from someone is a good way to push them toward burnout.

Most people don't consider these different trajectories and their overlapping effects on one another. Leadership in Nina's company likely didn't even consider that Nina's changed behavior at work is due to the extra demands of maintaining a healthy marriage and transitioning into parenthood. This sort of limited view is perpetuated by the myth of "work-life balance." Work, home, relationships, caregiving, and every other area of a person's life are all interconnected and affect one another. Leaders must understand this interconnectedness to make informed, values-aligned decisions for the good of their employees and organizations.

How Organizations Can Support Lifestyle Balance

Permeable, flexible boundaries are a reality of life, and they can work to the employee's benefit. However, *blurred* boundaries between an employee's work roles, their physical spaces, and their emotional lives are still the quickest way to burnout. Unpredictable scheduling expectations may stand in the way of being satisfied with their parental role. A toxic microculture at work might harm their emotional regulation, which may, in turn, do damage to their marriage. Misalignment between a company's behavior and the employee's moral compass may complicate that person's role as a person of faith. Since so much of an organization's policies are outside an employee's direct control, the employee role is often a sticking point for people who are trying to proactively balance their lives.

When an employee does the Balance Mapping exercise, looks at their various roles, and tries to decide what changes to make, they'll have an easier time seeing where work prevents them from achieving lifestyle balance. The bad news for organizations is that if those employees don't see any way to change the points of misalignment between their job and their other roles, they might conclude that their only option is to quit their job.

The most straightforward way to get a better understanding of how employees balance their lives is to bring the Balance Mapping exercise into the workplace. Leaders will be able to see, both in words and images, the varied roles an employee plays inside and outside the workplace. That way, they'll be able to work with employees to help them achieve their goals while bringing their lives into balance.

Adapting to the truth of people's lives outside work means greater success for individuals and the organization. Being more flexible with meeting and arrival times can help people balance work and caregiving demands. If a person is often distracted because they're grieving a loss, someone on their team can be assigned to check their work or assist with cognitively demanding tasks. The old model of telling everyone to "tough it out" because no one gets "special treatment" only causes low morale and high turnover (and burnout) rates.

The most successful, adaptable workplaces are the ones that are pioneering policies that take the employee's whole life into account. Organizations where employees thrive most adopt caregiver-friendly policies like flexible hours, paid parental leave, and robust benefits like health insurance, 401(k) matching, and student loan assistance.[1] They understand that encouraging wellbeing in areas outside of the actual workplace itself will make employees happier when they are at work, too. Greater satisfaction in one of their roles—employee—will lead to increased satisfaction in their other roles.

Acknowledging that lifestyle balance is vital for employee wellbeing means recognizing how interconnected every area of that employee's life is. It also requires leaders to always keep in mind how work impacts an employee's other roles and responsibilities in life. Using that information to its best advantage helps organizations develop and implement policies that suit their employees best, which in turn benefits adaptability. If organizations are adaptable to the varying seasons of their employees' lives, those employees become, in turn, more adaptable both in and out of the workplace. That's the true meaning of balance.

---

1. Kayla Webster, "How the Best Workplaces Make Workers' Lives Easier During Tough Times," *Inc.*, September 12, 2025. https://www.inc.com/kaylawebster/how-the-best-workplaces-make-workers-lives-easier-during-tough-times/91239270

8

Meaningful Participation and the Flow State

Over the last several chapters, I have established how individuals and workplaces should support employee efforts to protect boundaries, align themselves with company values, and create an ideal lifestyle balance for their particular situation. However, there is a key remaining element of workplace-related wellbeing: meaningful participation in the work itself. When leaders allow individuals to find meaning in their jobs, it sets a foundation for employee satisfaction. Leadership can mitigate toxic microcultures, always-on culture, and other blurred boundaries, even if it is a long and involved process. Even so, if an employee doesn't derive meaning from their work, their levels of satisfaction will sink lower and lower, and they will be more prone to burnout.

Meaningful participation forms the last letter of the BLOOM framework, but just because it's the last letter does not make it the lowest priority. Meaningful participation is essential for retaining employees without sucking the life out of them. It is the subjective factor that keeps employees coming back to work day after day. It can also result in "flow states," or periods of focus and enjoyment that can serve employees' mental and physical health with the byproduct of better outcomes in the organization itself.

The quality of life that results from proper lifestyle balance is about more than just clear boundaries and a lack of conflict around the office. It's about filling one's days with activities that a person looks forward to, or at least activities that facilitate their accomplishment of life goals. By valuing meaningful participation, an organization is less likely to lose people to burnout and will get to reap the benefits along with their employees.

Participation Is Not about KPIs

When some leaders see the word "participation," often their minds go straight to productivity and performance metrics. From the point of view of an employee, impressive performance metrics are not necessarily correlated with how much purpose they find in their jobs. High performance is an outward measurement of employees' work, quantifying how much they can accomplish in alignment with the company's goals. Employees who don't perceive their jobs as meaningful struggle to connect with their work. However, unless they're already burnt out, they can often do the work they need to earn their paycheck.

Meaningful participation, on the other hand, is an intrinsic experience, something that gives employees a reason to come to work every day. With meaningful participation, the individual fully engages with what they're doing and are one with it. They get a sense of purpose from their work, and that purpose replenishes their motivation day after day instead of draining their energy. These employees are also more likely to experience what's called a "flow state."

Flow is a concept introduced by philosopher Mihaly Csikszentmihalyi that describes a heightened state of engagement in an activity that makes people who are in it so absorbed they lose track of time. Flow states do encourage heightened productivity, as by definition they produce extreme focus. For example, professional athletes who perform at elite levels describe being "in the zone," another way of describing the flow state. Employees who reach flow states may, as a side effect, get more done in shorter amounts of time. They're more likely to reach benchmarks, as long as they're focused on work that is aligned with the organization's goals. However, performance doesn't define flow, nor does it guarantee an individual will derive meaning from their work.

Meaningful Participation Facilitates the Flow State

Flow states can emerge during the tasks that comprise a person's daily activities, whether they are work-related tasks or hobbies. One of my stress-relieving hobbies is putting together jigsaw puzzles. When I'm working on a jigsaw puzzle, I often become wholly focused on it and lose track of time. The flow state creates a space where I'm not tempted to look at my phone notifications or entertain anxious thoughts; I'm too focused on the activity itself to worry about those things.

Engaging in activities that produce flow is like a restorative treatment for the human mind. Flow is a powerful tool when it comes to overall wellbeing, a true method of self-care on par with meditation. In fact, flow is itself a form of mindfulness, which has been proven to decrease stress levels and calm the nervous system. When a person is in a flow state, they are not feeling stressed or hypervigilant, and so flow can act as a reset button for the brain that pulls individuals back from pre-burnout.

The more often a person can engage in work in a way that focuses their energy—that puts them into flow—the more likely they are to get satisfaction out of their jobs. A flow state provides a reprieve during a person's day where they're not staring constantly at the clock or getting distracted by office gossip or online shopping. It gives them an opportunity to center themselves; if before that point they'd felt like a stretched rubber band, flow states allow them to relax again. The more often they can achieve flow states, the less likely they are to become overstretched and the more likely they are to avoid burnout.

You cannot have a flow state without meaningful participation, and ideally, workers will feel enough purpose in their jobs to be able to regularly feel it. But remember, the flow state itself should not be the end goal of meaningful participation. While these two things can go together, employees finding meaningful participation in their work does not guarantee they will always enter a flow state. Like high performance metrics, it should be considered a fortunate byproduct.

Meaning Fuels Satisfaction and Focus

Meaningful participation looks different to different people whose jobs consist of different combinations of tasks. For some positions, the tasks may involve what would be considered mindless work: stuffing envelopes, data entry, or any other repetitive low-attention task. To others, more complex tasks like research and writing or interpersonal interactions like sales calls or human resource management are required. However, more often, it's a combination of many of these things. To be clear, meaningful participation in one's job isn't about the actual tasks one enjoys doing. It's an overall sense of alignment with the outcomes or effects of one's work.

Meaningful participation could mean a person goes to work every day so they can put their kids through school. The ability to provide for their children is what keeps them engaged with their day-to-day tasks. That does not mean every task they complete puts them into a flow state. While flow can be achieved within the context of individual tasks, those tasks cannot form the infrastructure of an employee's sense of purpose.

The person who stuffs envelopes every day might experience a meditative state just from that activity, but the relaxation found there is not sustainable enough on its own. Even for people who find that task enjoyable, it could become so repetitive one day that it no longer sparks pleasure. Whereas this employee used to enjoy the simple, systematic aspects of stuffing envelopes, one day a switch may suddenly flip. Instead of being a source of satisfaction, the task turns into an additional source of stress.

Why am I just putting paper in envelopes all day? What's the point? I hate my job!

From the perspective of Lifestyle Balance Mapping, losing a sense of meaning at work brings the satisfaction rating down to a much lower number than before. Since work doesn't stand apart from the rest of a person's life, a dip in an employee's work-role satisfaction affects the satisfaction they experience in different areas of their lives and lowers the employee's overall sense of wellbeing.

The key to making sure this doesn't happen is encouraging employees to develop a deeper meaning for why they do what they do. That meaning doesn't have to be a direct consequence of the actual tasks that a person is performing. It could be connected to the outcomes the organization produces (e.g., an individual who works for a nonprofit organization whose cause they deeply support). However, the meaning doesn't necessarily have to be an outcome of the work itself either. It can also apply to the employee's motivation and experience of doing the work.

Take the example from Chapter 5, where I discussed four people working in the call center of a larger organization whose microculture encouraged underperformance. Even though they were supposed to be making around twenty calls a day to schedule appointments, these call-center employees were only making an average of five each day. They didn't feel a sense of purpose; they were bored, distracted, and unmotivated to do their jobs.

Then, when their supervisor implemented a system of quotas, competitions, and incentives, it literally changed the game for these employees. Now that their work was gamified, making as many calls as possible held much more inherent appeal. Even if making the calls and appointments themselves wasn't a good enough incentive, friendly competition, active camaraderie, and potentially winning the prize of the week (typically a gift card) added meaning to the work they were doing. Now that their participation felt meaningful, they enjoyed themselves more, and as a consequence, they produced better results for the company.

It should be said that meaningful participation depends on the attitudes of the employees, and those attitudes can be affected by elements outside the work itself. If that toxic microculture had been strong enough to prevent new policies from being adopted, the employees would have remained out of alignment with the organization. If one employee didn't enjoy the game, they wouldn't have that new sense of purpose. Meaningful participation is subjective and varies from individual to individual. Sometimes, that may easily align with an organization's values, but whatever the case, it must align with the individual's values to instill them with purpose.

Purpose Steers Priorities

Meaningful work doesn't just apply to the tasks a person enjoys—actually, people who feel a sense of purpose in their jobs may hate some of the individual tasks they need to do. If someone is planning a birthday party for their spouse, they may really dislike the tedium of making reservations. They may find baking a cake to be difficult and exhausting, and they may hate the hassle of gathering RSVPs from friends. However, they are dedicated to completing all these tasks because they love their spouse and want to make them happy. Even if every task on that list is something the individual dreads, they find purpose in the project as a whole and will derive satisfaction from the outcome of all these tasks combined.

When I was doing my PhD, there were many tasks I enjoyed and found interesting and others that irritated me. For my research, I used grounded theory, which requires the researcher to collect qualitative data before even beginning to develop hypotheses (in this case, I conducted many interviews). It's not the same as a study where researchers start with a hypothesis and set up experiments to test it. This form of research tests the researcher's patience and ability to delve deep into work. There were tasks I liked, such as going back and listening to my interview recordings to pull out insights. Then there were the tasks I hated, like the tedious-but-assiduous task of coding those interview transcripts. The process was painful at times, but when I was doing tasks I disliked, I often reminded myself of the reasons behind all of them. Periodically taking stock of my priorities helped me stay persistent and focus on what needed to be done, even if I didn't like every component task.

On the other hand, the struggle to find meaning and purpose can reveal points of major dissatisfaction in a person's life. Regularly interrogating one's sense of purpose prompts individuals to weigh the pros and cons of the work they're doing. If they conclude that multiple parts of their work are making them unhappy, they are more likely to ponder whether their suffering is worth the outcome. If the reason isn't powerful enough, weighing pros and cons can help employees reorganize and reprioritize. An employee who dislikes the majority of the tasks they must perform should check in with themselves, then use the data they have gathered to gauge their level of satisfaction. Sometimes that means they stay the course, but sometimes that means they choose a new path entirely.

The Consequences of Short-Term Productivity Solutions

In earlier chapters, I've demonstrated how creating empty policies is an ineffective strategy for preventing burnout. It is easy to write catchy slogans and post inspiring statements on one's website, but those actions do nothing to increase employee trust or quality of life. Focusing on words alone disregards the reality of an individual employee's experience. It's only when an organization comes into alignment with its own values, as well as those of its employees, that meaningful change can occur.

Productivity metrics are short-term solutions that don't indicate employee health or wellbeing. Without alignment with organizational and employee values, those metrics are as cosmetic as a neglected flexible-hours policy, written in a handbook but never encouraged by leadership. You cannot assume just because someone is meeting productivity benchmarks that they are entering multiple flow states or coming into the office with a sense of purpose. Leaders who ignore their employees' wellbeing and don't give them opportunities to meaningfully participate will lose people to burnout and pay highly in both time and money to replace them, often repeatedly.

Consider the high turnover rates of junior employees in organizations. These are almost always the same people who receive lower pay, have less autonomy in decision-making, and get little to no opportunities for professional development. When they look at their futures at an organization, and they don't see the possibility to advance, they risk spiraling into burnout. On the other hand, if they are empowered to make decisions and take responsibility, they feel more in control because they know their job matters.

Tracking productivity metrics without considering whether an employee gets any satisfaction from their job leaves leaders not with indications of organizational health, but with new potential stressors. It takes much more cognitive effort to get things done when one doesn't feel that they're doing meaningful work. If the only reason employees are in a particular job is because they need income, an organization can easily lose them to another organization that offers more money and better benefits.

Getting assigned tasks that seem meaningless, tedious, or unenjoyable wears on an individual over time. Confusion over what that employee is actually supposed to be doing will also erode their sense of meaning. It's difficult for an employee to feel satisfied with their work when they are unsure whether they're doing the right thing. When the employee in question teeters on the edge of burnout after striving for KPIs in a position they find meaningless, they may take a moment to evaluate their priorities. If their combined tasks don't add up to something that instills a sense of purpose, or if they don't have the autonomy to make their job meaningful, they may decide that it isn't worth the trouble and quit.

How Organizations Can Encourage Meaningful Participation

Within an organizational setting, higher employee satisfaction means higher retention, and higher retention means more cohesive teams and a better organizational culture. Approaching burnout prevention through the lens of meaningful participation—not productivity metrics—meets people on a human level rather than a conceptual one. Instead of making it a problem-based approach, leaders take a wellness-based approach. Here are a few ways organizations can help employees ground themselves in meaningful participation.

First, **focus on "why."** When the metrics drop, don't reach for productivity hacks to get the numbers to go up again. This is a temporary solution. First, consider why employees may feel out of touch with their sense of purpose. Feeling stuck in a rut is a warning sign for impending burnout, and looking for creative solutions to help employees participate in a meaningful way at work is a more sustainable solution than simply pushing them harder.

Next, **empower employee decision-making**. When employees are required to turn to a higher-up for every single decision they make, it can make them feel like nothing more than a tool. If they're commanded to complete tasks in ways they disagree with, or ignored when they suggest alternatives, they lose a sense of ownership over their work. Giving employees autonomy over a reasonable percentage of their decision-making encourages connection to the outcomes of their decisions.

Once they have the autonomy to make decisions, leaders should **encourage accountability** in their employees. Many people are highly motivated by either a desire for success or a fear of failure (or, most likely, both). The natural result of allowing employees to make autonomous decisions is that they will want to see the results of their labor. When they maintain ownership of a task or series of tasks, they know their job matters, and it has an impact on the rest of the organization.

Lastly, **maintain alignment with your values**. Remember every piece of the burnout prevention framework is connected. Remove one piece, and the construction may fall apart. What your organization offers its employees must be worth what the employees invest in it. This means organizations must stay aligned with values, respecting emotional, physical, and role-related boundaries and encouraging lifestyle balance. All those elements will give employees room to do meaningful work without burning out due to toxic organizational culture.

An employee's level of satisfaction at work strongly depends on their sense of purpose and meaning. By making work a place where they feel like they're making an impact, leadership is directly encouraging better satisfaction and lifestyle balance. Meaningful engagement, when combined with the other principles in this book, is the final puzzle piece to an individual's workplace wellbeing and the wellbeing of the organization as a whole.

9

Cultures that BLOOM

By now, we've seen ample evidence of how the systems within an organization make a major impact on employees' lives. The model that many organizations implement, one that places all responsibility for wellbeing on employee resilience, is unpredictable and mostly unsuccessful. An organization that is consistent with its values, and who respects the needs and autonomy of its employees, will see better employee retention rates and more agility when change is necessary. That is good news for organizations, because it empowers leadership to make changes that truly promote sustainable growth.

Implementing systemic change creates success stories throughout an entire organization, no matter its baseline culture. In the previous chapters, I've told stories and reported successful statistics from my client companies and beyond, like the call center that saw improved morale and performance because leaders understood their microculture and played to its strengths or the way that promoting an employee who felt they had hit a career wall kept them from leaving the organization. Organizations renowned for their positive treatment of employees have created policies in response to the pressures of parenting, increasing inflation rates, and a growing need for financial literacy.[1] These examples prove that addressing factors that affect employees both inside and outside the workplace makes for thriving organizational cultures.

According to surveys of CEOs, an overwhelming majority (95%) agree that executives should be responsible for employees' wellbeing.[2] With the knowledge that better outcomes result from myriad combinations of systemic changes, leaders may feel stuck when trying to decide where to start. It's not a one-size-fits-all situation, so there will be nuances in the process for the organizational culture as a whole, for the multiple microcultures within the organization, and for each individual employee's situation. However, using my BLOOM framework to analyze their current culture, a leader can get an idea of where to begin improving their systems, plan for something better, and most importantly, embody the changes they want to see.

Follow The BLOOM Framework

The BLOOM Framework is an acronym that stands for burnout prevention, lifestyle balance, organizational culture, optimal quality of life, and meaningful participa-

---

1. Kayla Webster, "How the Best Workplaces Make Workers' Lives Easier During Tough Times," *Inc.*, September 12, 2025. https://www.inc.com/kaylawebster/how-the-best-workplaces-make-workers-lives-easier-during-tough-times/91239270
2. Deloitte, "New Research From Deloitte Finds C-Suite May Soon Join the Great Resignation, Uncovering Well-Being Is a Top-Down Organizational Concern," *PR Newswire*, June 22, 2022. https://www.prnewswire.com/news-releases/new-research-from-deloitte-finds-c-suite-may-soon-join-the-great-resignation-uncovering-well-being-is-a-top-down-organizational-concern-301572794.html

tion. This framework and its components set the standard for sustainable success in an organization. When building or adjusting a culture with each of these elements in mind, employees are more likely to maintain satisfaction in their work without becoming stretched until they snap. Here is an overview of the framework and its elements in the context of the previous chapters, accompanied by some thoughts on how these tools put leaders on the path to a more intentional culture.

A note: Not all of these questions are ones that leaders can answer without outside help, but they can act as starting points to diagnose issues and come up with possible solutions.

B - Burnout Prevention

BLOOM is an approach that starts from the top down with burnout prevention being the ultimate goal of adjusting organizational culture and systems. Burnout prevention is the outcome that every other element in the framework supports. Burnout is a culmination of events and inputs coming together to damage an individual's state of wellbeing. When burnout happens on a larger scale, it can also damage the organization as a whole. Preventing burnout requires various, customized methods. To diagnose their own organizational issues, leaders should start their evaluations at the top.

It's vital to remember that burnout is not a problem to be solved, nor is it completely within an individual's control. No matter how well-intentioned, individual interventions that only offer coping mechanisms are ineffective and can sometimes even put additional pressure on an employee. While everyone's experience of burnout is affected by individual factors like their personality traits, elements of their lifestyle, and their jobs, the only way to help a diverse range of people within an organization is to make systemic change.

When I start working with an organization, many of the employees are in a state of pre-burnout. Like rubber bands that are constantly stretched out, they are at risk of snapping. Employees on their way to burnout experience symptoms like excessive fatigue, headaches, irritability, and an inability to focus due to poor sleep. They're headed toward burnout, a state characterized by a feeling of depletion, cynicism, and emotional distance that results from a lack of impact or autonomy at work. Halting and slowing that progress toward burnout is vital to avoid employees "quiet quitting" or quitting altogether.

Starting Points for Leaders

The greatest key to burnout prevention is recognizing that it is not an individual problem, but one that is system-wide. Individual resilience is a factor, and looking at what employees face daily will help lessen the strain on them, no matter how high their tolerance level for pressure. Toxic work behaviors perpetuated by mismatched values between individuals, microcultures within the organization, as well as the organization as a whole, also house sources of burnout. Clues for where the causes of burnout may lie can be found in the answers to these questions:

- Are there discrepancies between what different individuals or departments report to leadership?
- Are multiple people not delivering the work they're supposed to have done, even if they look busy all the time?

- Are there groups that see one another as rivals and spread gossip or complaints about one another?
- Are people leaving the organization more quickly than they used to?
- Where and when does communication break down between individuals or departments?
- Is there a lack of enthusiasm among employees, demonstrated by decreased energy and low satisfaction?

One in four employees surveyed across various demographics and all over the world reported experiencing symptoms of burnout.[3] However, not every organization has to contribute to that statistic. Any organization can investigate the causes of pre-burnout and act accordingly to correct toxicity in the workplace and build a more supportive environment.

L - Lifestyle Balance

"Work-life balance" is a false dichotomy. Many employees spend much of their waking hours working at their jobs. Especially in a post-COVID world, many employees have more permeable boundaries between when and where they engage with work. "Work-life balance" implies that work and life are two separate things, and that is simply not the case.

The term "lifestyle balance" is a more accurate term for the way work interacts with other domains of a

---

3. McKinsey & Company, "What Is Burnout?" *McKinsey & Company*, August 14, 2023. https://www.mckinsey.com/featured-insights/mckinsey-explainers/what-is-burnout

person's life. Like the causes of burnout discussed in the previous section, life consists of overlapping domains that require varying levels of time and attention and ask an individual to perform different roles. These include roles as a caregiver, as a member of a family, as a leader or volunteer in the community, or in other hats that a person wears.

These roles are never static; they change throughout an individual's life. Sometimes an individual can spend large amounts of time focused on their role as an employee, while other times they may need to make space for transitions in their lives, whether that be getting married or divorced, caring for a newborn, grieving a lost loved one, or moving house. When leaders consider their work at an organization as a part of their employees' lives, rather than separate from them, it can help open their eyes to the amount of energy employees are able to devote to their jobs at a given time.

Starting Points for Leaders

If a leader wants to understand where employees are focusing their priorities, they might consider administering a Balance Mapping exercise as described in Chapter 7. However, it can be labor-intensive to complete these exercises, and leaders may not know what to do with the information once they have it. It can also put pressure on employees who already have a lot on their plates.

Whether or not leaders choose to administer the exercise itself, there are three areas around which leaders can examine their organization's culture. The central aim is to identify where organizational norms encroach on an employee's ability to live a full life. Specifically, where do either the spoken or unspoken norms of an organization blur the following boundaries?

- **Physical boundaries:** Are employees able to predict when and how they will be needed at work, or do they have to be "always-on," even away from their desks?
- **Emotional boundaries:** Are there sources of misaligned values, such as an implicit culture of overwork, that may be putting emotional strain on employees?
- **Role Fluidity:** Are employees confused about what's expected of them due to poorly defined roles and unclear responsibilities?

Employees have diverse personal needs, and the things that help them achieve lifestyle balance are just as diverse. Leaders should consider ideas such as flexible work arrangements, particularly ones that are caregiver-friendly, and/or remote work options, and then encourage employees to use them.

O - Organizational Culture

As part of the BLOOM framework, organizational culture is the core of creating change. It allows organizations to support each employee to live their values and thrive in cooperation with others. The goal is for leaders of an organization to determine what its values are and come into alignment with them. That means, rather than simply announcing their values and expecting change to happen on its own, they must first focus on embodying those values daily.

While each organization is unique, they usually lean more heavily toward one of the following categories: clan culture, hierarchical culture, adhocracy, or market-driven culture. Some organizational cultures may be more prone to practices that cause employees stress; for example, a clan culture may purport to take all team members' opinions into account when making decisions, but the norm may be that the owner runs the business like a dictatorship. A supposedly hierarchical culture may have neglected to properly define roles and responsibilities for all of their employees, crossing individuals' boundaries by playing into the myth of role fluidity.

However, while every organization can have its points of potential failure, they can also have areas where they are more likely to see success. Adhocracies and market-driven cultures can offer more opportunities for employee autonomy and the introduction of fresh ideas. Clan culture can be an excellent place to work for caregivers, due to its more democratic nature and sense of shared responsibility in community. Hierarchical cultures are more likely to provide clear boundaries between roles. Leaning into the best qualities of your culture will help you create an organization aligned with its values.

Starting Points for Leaders

Being aware of your organization's baseline culture will help you figure out how to move and pivot in a way that will work for you, not against you. Avoid the mistake of trying to act in opposition to the existing culture. For example, don't try to transform a competitive, market-based culture into a more rigid, hierarchical one, or don't let a clan culture fall into an adhocracy that blurs boundaries between roles and hamstrings employees' ability to unplug from work. Here are some questions to ask yourself when you begin to consider cultural changes:

- What type of culture forms the baseline for your organization (clan culture, hierarchical culture, adhocracy, or market-driven culture)?
- What are your organization's stated values and how do you measure up to them?
- In addition to the larger company culture, are there any microcultures where either implicit norms or explicit rules stand in the way of employee wellbeing?
- What populations (caregivers, people of color, people with disabilities, etc.) may experience unique misalignments due to norms at your organization?
- How will you communicate changes to leadership and employees in a way that affects true change?

In order to keep positive changes alive, there needs to be intentionality and accountability in leadership. Whenever an organization implements cultural changes, leadership must incorporate those changes into daily practice first—they need to walk the talk. Managers must be trained to model policies you want to catch on. Leaders must observe progress and revisit stated values on a regular basis to make sure leadership's behavior is in alignment with them. Above all, they must keep an open dialogue by creating a safe space for employees to give feedback.

O - Optimal Quality of Life

We've established that avoiding burnout requires that employees have space to create Lifestyle Balance. In order for them to be able to do that, organizations should do what they can to encourage optimal quality of life. This is an outcome that occurs when individuals are able to meet their needs both at work and away from it, including material needs, health needs (mental health included), and the time they need to address their responsibilities outside of work.

Most are dependent on the organization where they work as their only source of income, healthcare, a secure financial future, and more. When those benefits don't measure up to the cost of living, employees may be forced to do things like take on additional work or second jobs. Lack of flex time or time off incurs additional costs for caregivers (for many, the cost of childcare takes them out of the workforce altogether), and can cross emotional boundaries by causing guilt, shame, and anxiety. These stressors push them closer to burnout, which has negative repercussions throughout the organization. When one employee struggles, it hurts everyone, and chances are, when costs outweigh the benefits of working somewhere, an organization's retention drops.

It's not enough just to supply better pay. Employees should feel secure that when they come into work, they don't need to be on their guard. Addressing issues like toxic microcultures, conflicts within departments, and friction between individuals and groups of individuals will remove sources of unhappiness from an employee's workday.

Starting Points for Leaders

Leaders who pay attention to their employees' experiences are more likely to see where the organization fails to meet their needs. On a practical level, designing benefits and pay in a way that allows employees to balance their lives will help them relax rather than live in a state of constant tension, like the rubber band about to snap. Addressing the more complicated emotional struggles that take place within microcultures may be more difficult to address. However, if they are, employees will feel safer and more satisfied at work. Consider the following when evaluating your workplace's effect on employee wellbeing:

- Do the pay and benefits you offer align with the demands of the current state of the economy, adjusted for inflation?
- Are employees forced to take on additional jobs in order to afford housing and other basic needs?
- In what ways can you adjust your remote work, flexible hours, and time-off options to support caregivers, disabled people, and others going through life transitions?
- Have employees made complaints in your organization, and if so, how has the organization responded?

Examining issues such as internal conflict between departments and microcultures, and even between individuals, may pose a unique challenge for leaders. They may only encounter employees who are on their best behavior and feel too intimidated to give feedback. In those cases, it is often good to bring in an objective outside consultant (someone like me) to investigate.

M - Meaningful Participation

The foundation that holds up the previous elements in the BLOOM framework is meaningful participation. This is the outcome of every individual contributing to their organization in a way that plays into their skills and values. There is overlap between this state and the others, but meaningful participation is specifically defined as the sense of purpose and autonomy people feel in the workplace.

Even when work is challenging (or dull), meaningful participation allows individuals to see exactly how their actions and the outcomes they produce create alignment with their values. At the best of times, an individual who gets to do work that fits their skills, interests, and values will enter a flow state that keeps them fully engaged with the work they're doing. This gives employees an opportunity to relax from the tension they may often feel in the workplace, even as they do their work, which directly safeguards against burnout and its precursors.

Employees who feel a sense of purpose don't need to get it from individual tasks themselves. They can feel purpose from being part of a team working to accomplish something together, or they can feel it from knowing there is a possible promotion or bonus in their future. Autonomy in their work and decision-making, as well as accountability when they truly own their tasks, inspires a sense of purpose. If leaders create rewarding scenarios that encourage autonomy and accountability, it can go a long way to ensure employees feel that they are participating meaningfully in their jobs.

Starting Points for Leaders

Meaningful participation isn't about KPIs—it's about mental and emotional health. The result of more employees deriving meaning from work is evident in the way people engage, offer solutions, and feel satisfied with their work. Explore these questions to determine ways to help employees experience more meaningful participation.

- Are employees clear on what their roles and responsibilities are within the organization and their individual departments?
- Do employees get opportunities to voice their opinions and make decisions?
- Have you given employees space to be themselves and express their identities?
- Are employees getting opportunities to apply their individual strengths and skills to their work?
- Are positive outcomes celebrated at every level throughout the organization, so that everyone sees they played a meaningful part?

Meaningful participation keeps employees from coming into work and saying, "What am I even doing here?" Every task doesn't need to be exciting or even enjoyable, but if it's leading toward a greater purpose, you'll see more happiness from your employees and even positive business results.

Focus on Alignment, Not Numbers

An organization BLOOMs when its values align with employees' values, when employees' needs are being met, and when everyone is given a safe space to be themselves and apply their skills. Creating that culture can't be done in a single meeting or workshop, and it can't be checked off a list. Business KPIs and metrics aren't enough to measure the benefits of focusing on alignment; they should be a byproduct of building a healthier culture, not the main goal.

The best workplaces put health first and business outcomes second, although outcomes are often better at organizations where employees have better wellbeing. Keeping employees happy means they will be more engaged with their work and stay at the organization longer. By setting that foundation of meaningful participation, and by designing an organizational culture that encourages optimal quality of life and lifestyle balance, you're making burnout a much less likely outcome.

However, these evaluations aren't made one after another in alignment with the BLOOM framework, nor will the same solutions work for any two organizations. Even different departments and microcultures within the organization will require unique pivots and interventions. It is up to leadership to find ways to gauge what will make their employees' lives better and keep them happy in the workplace. That may take some experimentation, and it may require help from outside the organization, but when it causes your employees to show their brightest and best colors, the benefits are well worth the investment.

Conclusion: Culture as Leadership Strategy

If you are a conscientious leader, you likely picked up this book because you are trying to identify the cause of your organization's problems. Maybe employees or departments are giving you conflicting reports, but you are unsure whether that disconnect originates from individual disagreements or simply a lack of communication. Maybe some employees consistently fail to meet their productivity targets, and you can't put your finger on the reasons they're falling short. There is also the possibility that everyone is performing well, but you see high turnover rates or general signs of low morale. Maybe you haven't noticed these things for yourself but are concerned by reports from trusted members of your organization.

If you look more closely, symptoms will be evident in individual employees as well. Red flags might include overwhelm triggered by endless to-do lists, difficulty concentrating, and symptoms of physical exhaustion like fatigue, headaches, chest pains, and dizziness. While everyone has varying levels of stress tolerance, some may have limited bandwidth due to life transitions like growing their families, moving, or sending a child off to college. Some may simply be more prone to exhaustion or have conditions that make them more vulnerable to stress. Any of these effects can be responsible for the problems you see in your organization when you zoom out.

Leaders often have a hard time identifying exactly what is wrong. They have different priorities and responsibilities that keep them separate from their employees' day-to-day experiences. Unfortunately, I can confidently say that if you see these high-level consequences in your organization, a number of your employees are likely heading toward burnout. Once they reach the point of burnout, they may become cynical and disengaged. Unless something drastic changes, this may mean they emotionally disconnect from their jobs or quit altogether.

The good news is that as a leader, if you take proactive steps, you can pull employees back from the edge and help prevent these negative outcomes in the future. Taking those steps requires a mindset shift away from the myth of employee resilience and toward holistic, systemic change. To make change, you must remember these corrections to common false beliefs:

1. Burnout is *not* a reflection of weakness in an individual.
2. Burnout is *not* defined by an employee's lowered productivity.
3. Burnout is *not* a "problem" to be solved.

These false beliefs misguide many leaders into treating the symptoms of burnout rather than its root causes. "Stress reduction" workshops, lunchtime yoga classes, and similar types of individual interventions are self-defeating at best and harmful at worst. After all, if employees are in pre-burnout, adding an additional responsibility to their plate will only add one more task on their constantly growing list.

Now that you've read this book, you've hopefully stopped asking, "How do we help employees cope?" and instead are asking, "What systems are driving people to the edge in the first place?" If you've successfully shifted your mindset this way, congratulations! You are now ready to begin uncovering the unique issues causing burnout in your organization and to start adjusting your organizational design to promote employee wellbeing.

Organizational Design as Cause and Cure

Even when an organization's front-facing policies seem to encourage employee wellbeing, creating a working environment that prevents burnout requires digging deeper. An organization may advertise perks like flexible work-from-home options, it may proudly display its values on its website, and it may claim to encourage "work-life balance," a false dichotomy we've discussed throughout this book. Yet, if leaders don't lead by example, these professed values don't matter.

Burnout originates in misalignments. Often a portion of the misalignment issue reveals itself as a mismatch between an organization's professed values and how it operates. Even more harmful, and the most common reason organizations contract me, are misalignments between an organization's values and those of its employees. Solving this kind of misalignment requires discovering what employees value, whether that means dedicating more time to a caretaking role, unplugging from work at the end of the day without facing retaliation from a supervisor, or being encouraged and supported in bringing their true selves to work. That discovery is only the first step. Organizations must also follow through and communicate their commitment to bringing organizational norms into alignment with what employees value.

Studies have demonstrated that organizations that communicate their values every day through behavior, rather than just pronouncements, have higher rates of employee trust and engagement. In order to achieve positive outcomes, an organization's design must be reflected in the way its leaders behave. The results are obvious and show up in the organization's performance, overall morale levels, and the cohesiveness of teams and departments.

However, KPIs or growing productivity rates are not the point. They're merely a happy byproduct. As a leader, the way to improve both employee wellbeing and business outcomes involves addressing larger systems. Rather than focusing on an individual plant that isn't growing as it should, the best leaders understand that a healthy garden requires healthy soil, regular watering, sunlight, and feeding according to each plant type's specific needs. Similarly, coordinating multiple methods of burnout prevention can create an organizational culture that BLOOMs.

The A-E Method of Sustained Success

It's your responsibility as a leader to design and uphold your organization's values, but it can be tempting to reach for quick fixes. The work you are taking on isn't about a one-and-done diversity workshop or a new mission statement. Those things quickly fade into the background; without commitment to true change, the organization returns to its status quo. If you believe burnout is not a problem to be solved, it follows that reactive fixes aren't enough for an organizational culture to remain healthy over time.

Instead, the goal is to encourage meaningful participation while employees are at work and optimal quality of life for employees both inside and outside their working hours. Organizational cultural change is a means of creating an environment that allows an employee to have lifestyle balance. Only then can burnout be prevented. With the BLOOM framework in mind, here are five steps toward designing a culture that keeps employees satisfied and engaged for the long term.

Awareness

Be conscious of where you are embedded at the micro- and macro levels.

You can't know where you're going unless you know where you currently are, and that awareness starts with understanding the culture around you. It begins with knowing what type of organizational culture you have, whether that be clan, hierarchical, adhocracy, or market driven, and how those different types of cultures may overlap. Zooming in, it's also necessary to understand what microcultures exist within that greater culture and where every leader and employee exists within those structures. Role clarity is required when it comes to interconnectedness between an organization, its shifting microcultures, and the individuals that make up both.

The best leaders prioritize helping those in the organization communicate effectively around values, goals, and roles and responsibilities. Understanding these elements are vital to prevent burnout in an organization. When roles are unclear, some individuals are more prone to step in and take over tasks, while others are more likely to slack off and let their more proactive coworkers do their work for them.

When people are aware of what they are responsible for, it helps them avoid this trap. They also prevent miscommunication that can cause confusion within and between departments. A lack of awareness around workplace dynamics causes stressors that lower quality of life for employees. It pulls them away from having a sense of purpose in their jobs. When everyone has awareness of what surrounds them and how they fit into that structure, it's one more tool in the struggle against burnout.

Awareness also keeps businesses adaptable, and adaptability is vital for organizational success. For a leader, being aware of organizational culture at the highest levels and at the levels of microculture is key to identifying points of failure. For example, what happens when someone leaves the organization abruptly or takes time off? If a leader is aware of how each department functions, and they have successfully communicated so that everyone in the business shares a similar awareness, the remaining employees will be able to more quickly pick up the slack if they already understand what needs to be done and how they can help.

As a leader, your job is to make sure every employee understands how they fit into the organization. Frequently revisiting the way your organizational culture is communicated across departments keeps everyone aware of who you are as a company. It keeps you working together in pursuit of your collective goals.

Boundaries

Create limits to protect one's energy, time, and identity.

A person's boundaries can change according to their phase of life. Sometimes they are more rigid, like when a person is actively caring for a sick loved one. Other times, when they feel less pressure in non-work areas of their lives, boundaries can be more flexible. Allowing employees the autonomy to define their boundaries, and when and how those boundaries can change, is essential to their wellbeing.

To review, there are three types of boundaries that are constantly being negotiated and re-negotiated in a person's life. Those include physical boundaries, emotional boundaries, and cognitive boundaries around roles and responsibilities. Healthy boundaries are not rigid but permeable, meaning a person can control what is and is not allowed to pass through them. However, boundaries blur when an organization's values are out of alignment with their everyday practices. Those organizations tend to blur or even permanently delete boundaries without permission. This is likely unintentional, but sadly it is the reality of many individuals living with chronic stress due to juggling too many roles without any relief or support.

Blurred boundaries can show up in the way people set up their physical spaces—whether they only work at the office or a set space in their homes—and whether those boundaries are respected. "Always-on" culture blurs boundaries by making people think that wherever they are and whatever time of day it is, they must be hypervigilant and available to work. It also blurs emotional boundaries, as being on edge all the time takes a heavy physical and emotional toll.

"Always-on" culture isn't the only source of blurred boundaries. Blurred boundaries may also apply to how secure a person feels that there won't be any retaliatory actions if they speak freely about their work experiences. That is where leadership's behavior comes into play, as well as the behavior of other people working within a person's immediate environment. Toxic microcultures can keep employees from behaving according to their values, even if the organization itself does align with them. For example, an organization may say it values caregivers, but if a supervisor pushes back against a mom who needs to Zoom into a meeting so she can pick her kid up from school, that misalignment blurs an emotional boundary.

In the BLOOM framework, understanding boundaries is everything. In protecting them, an employee is able to make decisions about what passes through their boundaries and what doesn't. This enhances their quality of life and sense of autonomy while allowing them to experience meaningful participation in their work. As a leader, you must learn to respect boundaries and encourage employees to maintain them. Encoding them in the workplace handbook isn't enough.

That leaves the third boundary around roles and responsibilities, which also plays into the next step in sustained success. That boundary is impossible to understand without clear communication and regular affirmation from leaders.

Capacity

Prioritize work according to how much room is on your plate.

Often it doesn't occur to people that they can control their time. Whether it's from internal pressure, demands from superiors in the company, or simply from being so disengaged they'll accept anything that crosses their desk, many take an endless to-do list for granted. All work was due yesterday, and they don't even consider that they should take time to breathe. However, for both leaders and employees, choosing how and where to allocate time is an essential skill to avoid burnout.

Everyone has limited capacity when it comes to time and energy. You can't deny physics, no matter how much you might wish you could. To make the most of that capacity, employees must be able to focus on what is most important.

The first step is being able to identify what they are responsible for. The components that make up someone's role in a company must be clear, to the point that they come in every day knowing what tasks are at the top of their list. If they are pulled in multiple directions, or if they don't know who they are supposed to report to, it will show in the quality of their work. Eventually, it will also cause them to suffer frustration and edge them closer to burnout.

On top of role clarity, it's vital that employees have the autonomy to make decisions for themselves in order to correctly triage work within their capacities. That includes even–individuals at the lowest rungs of an organization. The ability to make decisions and be accountable for them helps employees find meaning within the organization. When they feel like they truly own their position, it encourages them to find meaningful participation in their jobs. However, it's not just about their ability to make decisions while they are clocked in; it's having enough clarity in their roles to make confident decisions outside of work as well.

This doesn't mean employees can do whatever they want and face no consequences. Good decision making and use of capacity comes from an awareness of one's responsibilities, parameters around behavior, and communication of boundaries. Individual decisions align with the organization's when the organization's values and expectations are clear. In a culture of burnout, employees can't make decisions without asking permission of a supervisor, often one that is overly critical and under-communicative, or they can't operate without being told exactly what to do. Without the autonomy they need to be successful, this kind of uncertainty in an organization leads to blurred emotional boundaries and the sort of stress that leads to burnout.

As a leader, the decisions you make to support organizational adaptability don't have to conflict with those you make to support employee wellbeing. They should instead lead to positive outcomes for everyone. Demoralized employees who feel that they can't make their own decisions are less likely to quickly adapt to the decisions leaders make. Staying adaptable as a business means keeping your team engaged, certain, and satisfied with what they do. It means everyone at the company, from the bottom up, sustainably thrives.

Daily Practices

Make a habit of self-care.

None of the A–E methods work in a vacuum, and the daily practices that individuals implement have everything to do with the capacity they have and the way they organize their tasks. No major change can happen all at once, which is important to remember when you're attempting to overhaul your organizational culture. Burnout prevention isn't the result of one sweeping, dramatic moment of change. It's in all the little things every person does day-to-day to achieve meaning and better quality of life. It's in the micro-changes in daily habits that break ineffective patterns of behavior over time.

This is where individuals make conscious choices to transform the way they approach work and life. At every level, people heal when they can intentionally take steps to make their workspaces healthier and more aligned with their values. Self-care applies to workplace practices as well as activities that are done at home.

These self-care activities may be related to the boundary protection we discussed earlier. For example, it may entail an employee, or a leader, turning off their phone and walking away from their desk at specific times of day. In the spirit of honoring one's capacity, it may mean saying no to projects or asking for extensions so the individual can be sure they've delivered their best work. It also means choosing to approach work in a way that maximizes meaningful participation and optimal quality of life.

Meaningful participation and healthy daily habits don't need to look the same for each employee, but leaders do need to give them clear opportunities for them to find these things. There should be ample opportunity for employees to achieve flow states at work, doing work that exercises their skills and feeds their brains. Making a daily habit of working in this way directly enhances wellbeing and works in direct opposition to burnout.

Enhanced Living

Bring fulfillment, wellbeing, and purpose together in a rhythm that reflects your deepest values.

Implementing policies, then really standing behind them, leads individuals to find more effective balance in their work and lives. Employees who feel that their efforts are well-placed are more likely to come into work with the energy they need to engage. Emotional safety through upheld values and clarity of expectations lead to a happier workplace, and that happiness leads to stronger performance.

When employees know where they stand and have a sense of purpose, they are much more likely to find the flow state at work. They can feel hours pass by like mere minutes as they pour their best energy into a project they feel invested in. Having these periods of full engagement, unbroken by role confusion and interpersonal conflict, is a source of stress relief. Flow states are often experienced the same way as mindfulness meditation, which is a proven method to increase wellbeing. Whether or not any particular employee reaches a flow state, though, a sense of purpose and a healthy work environment reduce stressors and can help reverse hypervigilance and fatigue.

The metaphor of individuals as rubber bands is often misunderstood. In too many work environments, individuals are expected to stretch and stretch without breaking, no matter their circumstances. What leadership often forgets is that rubber bands can't stay stretched at all times without eventually snapping. In any event, a rubber band that doesn't have the resources to return to its original form before being stretched again will become misshapen or deformed in some way.

Burnout has less to do with the person's capacity to stretch than the pressure their organizations place on them to keep stretching, constantly, with no regard for long-term consequences. The responsibility to ease the stretch and allow for a gentle rebound lies within organizational culture. No one can thrive in a state of never-ending tension.

It is your duty as a leader, both to your employees and to your organization, to create a healthy environment that allows for lifestyle balance. By defining and upholding values, you create space for employees to find their purpose. This might take the form of well-articulated and affirmed benefits like flexible work arrangements, paid leave, or employee resource groups. It could mean addressing conflicts within a department's microculture. Or it may require you to establish more concrete roles or pathways to promotion within your organization. Whatever the key is, creating an environment for enhanced living results in sustainability and adaptability for all involved.

Finding What Works for Your Organization

Cultural realignment is far from easy. It requires intentional investment in discovering what is going wrong and how to change direction in an effective way. That is not a one-size-fits-all situation, and it doesn't stop at recognizing burnout within your organization.

Most leaders waste far too much time and money guessing at the problems in their organization. They are often too close to the situation, so they fail to recognize problems that are obvious to a trained expert. In my experience working with organizations of all sizes and across many industries, a combination of expert training and outside perspective can save companies tens of thousands of dollars, making the investment in a cultural consultant a no-brainer. To access free resources on how to implement the BLOOM model in your organization, or to connect with me directly, visit luminousconnections.net. I look forward to helping you create a practical plan to pull your employees back from the brink of burnout and make your organization BLOOM.

Acknowledgments

My parents have built and run their own successful business for almost forty years. The foundational knowledge I gained about the everyday struggles and triumphs of leaders and employees helped me dive deep into burnout and its effects.

My sister, who I look up to for her love of books, inspired me to write what I am passionate about. My brother-in-law provided his unwavering support and insights from the world of start-ups.

My wife has believed in me from the very start of this journey. It was around 2012 when I first talked about writing a book. She knew it would happen one day and has stood by me every step of the way.

My two toddlers have taught me the true meaning of patience and kindness. In their name, I am committed to selfless service.

About the Author

Dr. Chetna Sethi is the founder and CEO of Luminous Connections. Frequently recognized for Lifestyle Balance Coaching and parenting expertise, she holds a PhD from University of North Carolina at Chapel Hill. Dr. Sethi has worked as an occupational therapist, a university professor, and a community partner. She has presented and written on the topics of Burnout Prevention and Cultural Change for over 20 years. She enjoys reading, traveling, and Pilates, and lives in Maryland with her family.

www.ingramcontent.com/pod-product-compliance
Lightning Source LLC
Chambersburg PA
CBHW052031030426
42337CB00027B/4954